Stokes
Purple Martin
BOOK

Stokes Nature Guides

by Donald Stokes

A Guide to Nature in Winter
A Guide to Observing Insect Lives
A Guide to Bird Behavior, Volume I

by Donald and Lillian Stokes

A Guide to Bird Behavior, Volume II
A Guide to Bird Behavior, Volume III
A Guide to Enjoying Wildflowers
A Guide to Animal Tracking and Behavior

by Thomas F. Tyning

A Guide to Amphibians and Reptiles

Stokes Backyard Nature Books

by Donald and Lillian Stokes

The Bird Feeder Book
The Hummingbird Book
The Complete Birdhouse Book
The Bluebird Book
The Wildflower Book — East of the Rockies
The Wildflower Book — From the Rockies West

by Donald and Lillian Stokes/Ernest Williams

The Butterfly Book

by Donald and Lillian Stokes and Justin L. Brown

Stokes Purple Martin Book

Stokes Field Guides

by Donald and Lillian Stokes

Stokes Field Guide to Birds: Eastern Region
Stokes Field Guide to Birds: Western Region

Stokes Beginner's Guides

by Donald and Lillian Stokes

Stokes Beginner's Guide to Birds: Eastern Region
Stokes Beginner's Guide to Birds: Western Region

By Donald Stokes

The Natural History of Wild Shrubs and Vines

Stokes
Purple Martin
BOOK

*The Complete Guide to
Attracting and Housing
Purple Martins*

Donald and Lillian Stokes
and Justin L. Brown

Little, Brown and Company

Boston New York Toronto London

First Edition

Library of Congress Cataloging-in-Publication Data
    Stokes purple martin book : the complete guide to attracting and housing purple martins / Donald and Lillian Stokes and Justin L. Brown. — 1st ed.
        p.   cm.
    ISBN 0-316-81702-3
    1. Purple martin. 2. Bird attracting. I. Stokes, Lillian Q. II. Brown, Justin L. III. Title.
    QL696.P247S76   1997
    598.8'26 — dc21   96-46179

10 9 8 7 6 5 4 3 2 1

Design and electronic production by Barbara Werden Design

RRD-OH

Published simultaneously in Canada by
Little, Brown & Company (Canada) Limited

Printed in the United States of America

Photograph Acknowledgments
Animals/Animals — C. C. Lockwood: 7, 58
Jen and Des Bartlett: 88
Steve Bentsen: 65
Justin Brown: 14, 16, 20
Rob Curtis/The Early Birder: 28, 52, 60, 61, 75, 79
Richard Day/Daybreak Imagery: 54
Bill and Pat Dietrich: 47, 48, 49, 50
Harold Lindstrom: 35, 87
Maslowski Photo: 42 bottom, 90, 91
C. Allan Morgan: 89
John Nisley: 21, 45, 77, 78
Hugh P. Smith, Jr.: 40 bottom, 67
Lillian and Don Stokes: 1, 6, 9, 10, 12, 13, 17, 18, 19, 22, 23, 24, 26, 27, 29, 30, 32, 33, 34, 36, 37, 38, 39, 40 top, 41, 42 top, 43, 44, 51, 56, 62, 63, 64, 66, 68, 69, 70, 71, 72, 73, 74, 76, 80, 81, 82, 83, 84, 85, 86, 90, 92, 93
John L. Tveten: 53, 55, 59
Tom Vezo: 31, 57

Contents

The Joys of Purple Martins

Becoming a Martin Landlord

It is hard to match the excitement of the sights and sounds of an active Purple Martin colony. Cheerful calls fill the air; dark purple birds gracefully swoop and soar as they fly, their wings and bodies forming streamlined silhouettes against the sky. And the hub of all activity is the house, with birds fluttering about, perching on roofs and porches, and busily going in and out of nest holes. These are the wonderful sensations of a colony, but they are just a few of the many reasons people are so fond of martins.

In addition, people love the challenge of attracting these beautiful birds. Every "landlord" does it a little differently, and there is lots of room for innovation and personal creativity. This can lead to many delightful hours of tinkering with your own colony.

Once you have attracted martins, there is also the exciting firsthand experience of witnessing the birds' lives as you monitor your colony and track the development of the young from eggs to successful fledglings.

When you become a Purple Martin landlord, you join millions of other people who try to attract these birds and provide them with homes. Part of the fun of the hobby is meeting this wide variety of people — young and old, retired and employed, people who live among the manicured lawns of the suburbs and those living at the ends of country roads, far from the nearest convenience store. All of them have one thing in common — their passion for these exquisite birds.

Sometimes people's love of the birds spreads further than just the care and maintenance of their own colony and they become Purple Martin ambassadors, spreading the good news about martins to neighbors or acquaintances who might not otherwise be exposed to these birds, especially children. Showing other people your colony and sharing your experiences is an excellent way to do this. There are clubs, national societies, and even Web pages on the Internet all devoted to Purple Martins and to helping people share their thoughts and ideas on this absorbing hobby.

There is one more very important point about attracting and caring for Purple Martins. East of the Rocky Mountains, Purple Martins nest almost exclusively in housing provided by humans; they rarely nest in the wild. These eastern Purple Martins prob-

A proud martin landlord with his colony.

A rainbow giving good luck to a Purple Martin colony.

ably cannot survive without our help. Practically no other wild animal in North America has such a close association with and dependence upon humans. Thus, providing housing for Purple Martins is not only fun and rewarding for us, it is also a virtual necessity for the survival of this species. Being a Purple Martin landlord is an act of conservation.

About This Book

This book is designed for everyone interested in Purple Martins, from beginners who may have never even seen a Purple Martin to experienced landlords who have been raising hundreds of successful fledglings for decades.

The body of the book has four sections. The first tells you everything you need to know to successfully attract martins. The second section details the lives and behavior of Purple Martins from the time the first bird shows up in spring, through all of their marvelous breeding behavior, to when the last bird leaves to winter in South America. In the third section, you will learn the many things you can do to monitor and help your colony during the breeding season. And finally, the last section tells how Purple Martins differ in the West, describes the history of Purple Martin colonies, and lists resources for Purple Martin supplies and societies.

Acknowledgments

Many people helped us on this project. We want to thank Andrew Troyer, Dave Fouts, Tom Dellinger, Ed Donath, Don Wilkins, and Carlyle Rogillio, as well as Louise Chambers and James R. Hill III of the Purple Martin Conservation Association, for the generous gift of their time and expertise. We want to thank Bill Dietrich for reading the manuscript and helping us see and photograph some superb martin colonies in Florida. And we want to give a special thanks to Terry Suchma for her continual guidance, careful reading of the manuscript, and contribution of the chapter Adverse Weather and Martins. We also salute her lifelong dedication to the education of Purple Martin landlords and the welfare and survival of the birds.

In a final note, Don and Lillian would like to thank their son, Justin Brown, for doing much of the research and writing of this book. Over the course of the project it was wonderful to see how easily the Purple Martins made their way into his heart.

We wish all of you the best of luck with your martins and hope that you will become enthusiastic advocates for the conservation of these wonderful birds.

Don and Lillian Stokes
Justin Brown

Purple Martin Basics

Getting Started

To help you get started, here is a brief overview of Purple Martins — their identification, behavior, and habitat needs. It is a good quick reference for the basics of martins.

Identifying Purple Martins

Purple Martins are the largest member of the swallow family and the only species of martin in North America. They spend most of their time flying, alternating soaring with brief flaps of their wings. When they are not flying, they are usually seen perched on the martin housing. They generally look all dark when seen against the sky, but there are some subtle differences between the sexes and ages that you can look for.

Adult Male — The adult male is all dark; his wings and tail are black, and his body is iridescent purple but can appear black in some lights. Males first acquire adult plumage during their third summer; thus, males with adult plumage are at least 2 years old.

Adult Female — The adult female is easily distinguished from the male because she is lighter colored. Her breast and forehead are grayish and her belly is whitish; her crown and back are purplish and her wings and tail are black. If you look closely, you will notice that the feathers under the base of her tail (the undertail coverts) are white with gray centers. Females with this plumage are at least 2 years old.

Subadult Male — In his second summer (first breeding season), a 1-year-old male looks like a subadult female, except that he has a dark throat and patches of purple feathers, either singly or in groups, on his breast and/or belly.

Subadult Female — In her second summer (first breeding season), a 1-year-old female looks like the adult female except for one subtle difference. The undertail coverts are all white, while in adults they are white with gray centers.

Feeding

Purple Martins feed while flying, usually hundreds of feet in the air. They often feed in loose flocks. They eat airborne insects, such as flying ants, bees, wasps, flies, midges, beetles, butterflies, moths, dragonflies, damselflies, and mayflies. Only about 3 percent or less of their diet is mosquitoes. Basically, if it flies and is an insect, then it is part of the Purple Martin's diet.

Nesting

In the eastern part of their range, extending northwest into Alberta, Canada, martins nest almost entirely in human-made housing — either conventional multicompartment houses or groups of gourds. Western populations of martins nest in natural cavities in trees, rock crevices, or saguaro cactuses, and, in the Northwest, occasionally in single-unit birdhouses and gourds, or in building crevices such as roof tiles.

In a compartment or cavity, martins build a shallow nest of small sticks, twigs, bark strips, pine needles, or grasses and add a lining of green leaves. They often construct a mud wall at the front edge of the nest, just inside the cavity entrance.

An adult male Purple Martin. Note the deep purple iridescence of the body and the black on the wings.

An adult female Purple Martin. Note the grayish breast and the gray centers of the feathers under her tail (undertail coverts).

A subadult male Purple Martin. He is similar to the subadult female, except he has blotches of dark feathers on his breast and/or belly.

A subadult female Purple Martin. Note her lighter appearance than the adult female and the all-white feathers under her tail (undertail coverts).

Breeding

Adult female martins lay 5–7 white eggs, with 5 the average. Subadult females lay 3–5 eggs. Incubation is done by the female only, and the eggs take 15–17 days to hatch. The nestling period (the time the young are in the nest) is 25–31 days. The fledgling period (the time the young are out of the nest but still fed by the parents) lasts 5–8 days. Purple Martins raise one brood per year.

Habitat

Martins inhabit open areas, usually near water. Open suburban yards and parks, farms, open wetlands, river valleys, and coastal areas are favorite habitats. The checklist on page 17 outlines habitat factors to consider in putting up colonial housing for martins.

Voice

Martins have many vocalizations. Their most common call is the easily recognized "cher-cher" call, heard constantly around the colony. They also frequently give their guttural, liquid song, which when given by the male ends in a grating sound.

An adult female martin looking out over the colony site.

Purple Martin Breeding Timetable

Here is an overview of Purple Martins' lives during the breeding season. The activity you will see is in boldface type, followed by a description of the breeding stage and the length of time this phase lasts.

Birds First Arrive — The first birds to arrive at the colony are adults. (See map, page 25, for approximate arrival dates in various parts of North America.) They may stay or leave temporarily, depending on weather and availability of food. In some locations, especially in the North, birds may leave the colony site for many hours each day to feed elsewhere. This behavior can continue for the first few weeks after arrival. In these cases, the birds will be seen at the colony mostly in the early morning and late afternoon.

Males and Females Enter Nest Holes — Soon after they arrive, males start to claim nest holes and sing to females. There may be fights among males over ownership of nest holes. As birds start to pair, females will enter nest holes of males. This period lasts 3–4 weeks.

Birds Carry Nesting Material to the Nest — About a month after the birds arrive, nest building starts. Birds gather grasses, twigs, and mud. It is done mostly by the female and lasts 3–4 weeks.

Subadults Arrive — Young birds now begin to show up at the colony. These are the birds that hatched the previous summer. Some of them will breed this summer, some will not. In either case, subadults play important roles in the social life of the colony.

Green Leaves Are Carried to the Nest — You will begin to see martins carrying green leaves to the nest. This activity continues from slightly before the start of egg laying until the end of incubation. One egg is laid each day, and egg laying takes 4–7 days, depending on the number of eggs laid.

The Female Is On the Nest for Long Periods — This is a sign of the incubation phase. Incubation starts after the next to last egg is laid, and it is done only by the female. It lasts 15–17 days.

Parents Bring Food to the Nest — When you see both parents repeatedly making brief trips to the nest, sometimes with food visibly in their bills, this is a sign that the young have hatched. As the young get older, they are brought larger food items. This phase lasts about 4 weeks.

The Young Are Out of the Nest — This is the start of the fledgling phase, when the young are fed by the parents outside the nest. It lasts about a week. After this phase, the young martins are independent of their parents and ready to join in premigration activities.

Birds Gather in Large Flocks — Large numbers of martins are seen perched on telephone wires, antennas, or trees. This indicates the birds are near the time when they will migrate south for the winter. Migration starts as early as June and July in the South and continues through October, when most Purple Martins have left North America.

Successfully Attracting Martins

How Easy Is It?

Some people seem to attract martins as soon as they put up the houses, while others wait years before they attract their first martins or, in some cases, never get martins at all. Is there any rhyme or reason to this?

It is impossible to say with certainty what circumstances attract Purple Martins. However, there are many ways that you can maximize your chances of getting martins. Some of these involve the housing itself; others involve the placement of the housing. And sometimes it is just luck!

Here are the best tips for putting your martin housing in a situation that will be most attractive to the birds.

Attract Subadults

If you are a first-time landlord, the birds that you are most trying to attract are called subadults — birds that hatched last year and do not yet have adult plumage. This is because these are usually the only martins that will start a new colony. Adult martins may colonize a new site if, for some reason, their old site is no longer suitable (for example, if it was preyed upon or has become crowded by trees), but they usually return to the colony where they successfully bred the previous year.

Subadults return later than adult martins. The migration map on page 25 is generated from the average return dates of the first adult birds to established sites. Subadults, on the other hand, return at least 4–6 weeks after these birds, and continue to arrive for another 4–6 weeks in the North and another 10–12 weeks in the South.

Martins nest near humans. In fact, if housing is more than 100 feet from human activity, martins may not use it.

If You Live in the West . . .

There is a big difference in nesting behavior between martins found east of the Rocky Mountains and those found farther west. The strategies for attracting martins to colonial housing described in this chapter and the next apply only to the birds east of the Rockies. If you live in the West, turn to Western Purple Martins, page 88, for tips on attracting and enjoying martins in your area.

Martin housing should always be in the open, at least 40 feet from tall trees or structures.

Thus, the period for attracting subadults to a new colony starts about 6 weeks after the first adults arrive in your area and lasts for at least a month.

Location, Location, Location

When putting up a martin house, there are three important things to consider: the breeding range of Purple Martins, the nearness of feeding areas, and the environment in the immediate area of the colony.

Breeding Range — Before buying housing, you should first see if you live in an area of the country where Purple Martins breed. To find this out, look at the map on page 15, which shows where Purple Martins breed in summer. In winter, Purple Martins leave North America and fly to South America.

If you live east of the Rocky Mountains, you have a good chance of attracting them. This is because eastern martins now nest mainly in human-supplied housing; they rarely nest in the wild.

If you live in the Northwest and within the martin's breeding range, you may be able to attract them to single-unit houses and/or gourds. However, Purple Martins are not common in this region. If you live in the Southwest, where martins usually nest in cavities in saguaro cactuses, attracting martins to artificial housing is unlikely to be successful.

Feeding Areas — Adult Purple Martins need lots of food in order to support themselves and feed their young. They eat only insects caught in the air and need large open spaces where insects are abundant. These areas include meadows, farms, marshes or swamps, ponds, lakes, creeks, rivers, reservoirs, and bays. In general, martins also can find enough insects in open suburban habitats to survive and raise young.

Placing your martin house in or next to one of these habitats is ideal but not essential. This is because martins can travel 1–2 miles from their nesting site to a feeding area.

Both rural areas and suburban residential areas offer good Purple Martin habitat. Waterfront property, whether on a pond, lake, canal, or the ocean, or along an open river, is also attractive to martins. Although your chances of attracting martins improve when you are adjacent to a body of water, this is not a necessity.

The only areas that Purple Martins seem to stay away from are heavily forested areas, exposed elevated spots like mountaintops, and densely populated metropolitan areas with few green spaces.

In addition to placing martin housing in the open, the landlord should keep the area at its base clear of bushes, vines, or any other brushy vegetation.

Although attracting martins to cities might be difficult, if there is open space and adequate insect life, give it a try. Placing colonies in public places, such as larger city parks, where many people would see them, is an exciting idea and should not be discarded just because martins have traditionally shunned cityscapes. Midwestern cities, which tend to be more spread out and have more open spaces than their eastern counterparts, sometimes offer prime martin habitat.

The Immediate Area Around the Colony — If you live within the range of the Purple Martin and near open habitat as described above, you are two-thirds of the way to attracting these lovely birds. Having the right kind of habitat for the colony itself is also very important.

It is generally accepted that there should be nothing taller than the Purple Martin housing within 40 feet of it. Martins prefer to have a direct flight path to and from their nest compartments so they can come in quickly to avoid aerial predators, like Sharp-shinned Hawks or falcons.

Purple Martin housing should be placed in as open a spot as possible. This means that the area immediately surrounding the colony should be free of trees, tall shrubbery, or any other tall structures. The birds tend to stay away from housing that is in a congested area, for any flight approach would mean slowing down and becoming an easier target for predators.

In addition, the bottom of the pole should be kept completely void of foliage. Any vegetation — tall grass, shrubbery, et cetera — around the base of the colony tends to scare off potential inhabitants, possibly because it would offer prime concealment to predators.

Contrary to what most people might think, martins seldom use housing placed in isolated spots, even if this is open habitat. Over the years, martins have learned that living near humans is ultimately safer and results in less predation than if they were in more remote locations.

Therefore, Purple Martin housing should be within 100 feet of human housing of some type. This includes houses and other structures, even if they are deserted, as well as roads, cars, docks, boats, and pedestrian traffic. Do not worry if you think an area might be too busy for the birds, for they have shown themselves surprisingly tolerant of even the loudest and most disruptive traffic and noises.

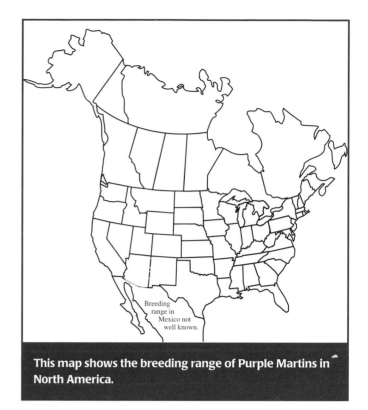

Breeding range in Mexico not well known.

This map shows the breeding range of Purple Martins in North America.

Guy wires should never connect to the Purple Martin housing from other structures or from the ground. This would offer some predators, such as raccoons, easy access to the colony. Even though martins love to perch on wires, it is best if the birds go to nearby power lines instead. Wires strung between two or more different martin houses so that gourds may be hung are okay.

Maintaining Your Purple Martin Habitat — It is important that once you attract Purple Martins, you keep them. This means being sure that the factors that make your particular site attractive — low trees, open space, and clear ground — stay as they are. Monitoring the vegetation each year around your colony location to make sure that no shrubs or trees are encroaching on the Purple Martin housing is extremely important.

Attracting Tips

In addition to offering martins the best housing and colony site possible, there are several things that you can do to encourage martins to visit your site.

If you live within a mile or two of several other active colonies, these may not be necessary. But those of you who live in areas where martins are less

One of the best ways to attract martins to your site is to play a recording of dawnsong. A simple cassette recorder can be used to play the tape early in the morning.

common — in New England, for example, or on the fringes of the martin's breeding range — may find these tips worth investigating.

Dawnsong Tape — The dawnsong is a vocalization given by adult males at established colonies in the hour or two before the sun rises. It is believed that this song serves to attract migrating subadult martins to the colony site. Playing a recording of this song at your unestablished site is an excellent lure for colony-hunting martins. (Tapes of Purple Martin dawnsong are available through the Purple Martin Conservation Association and Natural Insect Control. Refer to the Resources section at the end of the book.)

Because this song is thought to attract *subadult* martins — the primary birds that will come to unestablished colony sites — this tape needs to be played only when subadult martins will be coming through your area. To determine this, refer to the beginning of this chapter.

Playing the tape early in the morning, between 3:30 and 6:30 A.M. is best; some landlords have had

success playing it at other times of day as well. The easiest way to play the tape is to use a timer to turn a cassette recorder on and off. If the machine does not have an endless loop function, you can buy a loop tape at a nearby electronics store and record the dawnsong onto it.

Any cassette recorder, from a portable one to a home stereo component, will do the trick as long as it can play loudly without distorting the song. The acoustics of early morning are superb — due to moisture in the air and little wind disturbance — so the volume does not have to be set too high, just at the level of other early-morning birdsong. In general, playing dawnsong will not affect your sleep or that of your neighbors, for it blends in with the sounds of other birds singing.

Dawnsong can also be played during the last 3–4 weeks of the season before the birds leave. At this time, play it during the day, since adults and young are flying about and may visit other colonies as they explore future options.

Keep Holes Plugged Until Martins Arrive — Keep the entrance holes to your martin housing closed until the first birds arrive. Many commercial manufacturers sell caps that press into the holes and make this easy. The reason for this is to keep House Sparrows and European Starlings from using the compartments for roosting or early nesting, or in any other way getting established in your martin housing. When you see martins arrive in your area, open the holes. If you are attracting martins for the first time, open only as many holes as are needed for the number of birds you have attracted. In other words, if you have only 4 male martins that have arrived at a 12-compartment house, open about 4–6 holes. If more martins show up, open more.

When the season is over and all Purple Martins have left, around October, plug up the holes for the winter.

Additional Holes — The dark holes of multicompartment houses already provide a visual superstimulus to martins, so why not add a few more? Do not drill or puncture holes in your house or gourd, but draw or tape black circles onto the sides. This super-superstimulus might seem a bit much, but the end result is worth it.

Mud — Making the compartments seem used is another strategy. Martins may feel "safer" about using housing that looks like it has been used before, so any remains of a nest signals to them that other martins have been there. The best and most fun way to do this is to build a low mud wall in each cavity just inside the entrance. Splattering mud on entrance holes and porches will also do the trick. A few pine shavings (not sawdust and not cedar shavings) or pine needles in the nest may also help make the nest cavity look previously used.

Purple Martins Are Highly Compatible Neighbors

Many prospective landlords are afraid to attract martins to their property for fear something else will be pushed out. This never happens. Purple Martin colonies are compatible with just about any backyard endeavor, from other nest-box users to butterfly gardens.

Other nest-box users, such as Tree Swallows,

A gourd colony. These gourds have been outfitted with rain canopies to help keep the nests inside as dry as possible.

bluebirds, and House Wrens, as well as beehives, bats, and other backyard activities, can all peacefully coexist with Purple Martins. Martins were once mistakenly considered bad for areas with beehives, for they were thought to eat the bees. In most cases, Eastern Kingbirds were actually eating the bees and being mistaken for female martins.

Is It Too Late to Put Up Housing?

Even if you are convinced that the martins in your area have already passed through and you will not get any that season, you should still put up housing. There is a slight chance you might get some stragglers. You might even get a group of investigating martins from nearby colonies over for a short visit. The more aware the birds are of your colony's presence, the better.

A Checklist of Good Purple Martin Habitat

1. Make sure you live within the summer (breeding) range of Purple Martins. Check the map on page 15 as a reference.

2. Check to make sure there is adequate open feeding habitat within 1–2 miles of the colony. Although martins will travel a mile or more to find insects, they will not travel farther. Living near water is a major attractant, though not a requirement.

3. Make sure the housing is in the best location possible. This generally means being at least 40 feet from tall trees or structures and within 100 feet of human buildings.

4. Prevent any dense or high vegetation from growing around the base of the colony.

5. Do not allow any wires to connect the housing to other structures or to the ground; these could allow squirrels or predators to reach the housing.

Choosing Purple Martin Housing

Figuring Out What Is Best for You

If you are trying to attract martins for the first time, think small. It is not necessary to go out and buy an expensive, large multiunit house if you have no experience managing a colony or no idea whether or not you can attract martins.

An inexpensive, 12-compartment house with some gourds is a good starting point. If you want to buy commercially available housing, this setup can be bought for a little over $100, including a pole.

An adult female Purple Martin on a perch. Although not considered part of their breeding territories, perches are enjoyed by Purple Martins and are where large numbers of birds preen, sun, and loaf.

You can also start with just gourds for even less money, but including a house will increase your chances of attracting martins, especially when you are not close to other colonies.

It is not yet understood why martins prefer one type of housing over another. It has been proven that the type of housing they were raised in does not directly determine which kind they will choose to breed in. Therefore, offering a variety, such as gourds and houses, will increase your chances.

You can also build your own housing inexpensively. If you want to do this, simply look at what specifications are best for the martins and what building materials have proven themselves over time. See the section Building Your Own later in this chapter.

Different Kinds of Housing

Despite the large number of lines and models of commercially available housing, there are basically three different kinds of housing for Purple Martins: aluminum houses, wooden houses, and gourds. There is a lot of debate about which type is best for the birds, which will yield the most young, which is best for keeping out parasites and predators. Each kind of housing has its advantages and disadvantages. This section outlines all these differences and will help you understand the benefits of each type of housing.

Aluminum Houses

Aluminum houses first became available in large numbers in the 1960s. These houses are low-maintenance, durable, easy to use, and often fairly inexpensive. The big plus with aluminum houses is that they are lightweight and, therefore, easy to raise and lower on telescoping poles or poles with winching

A site that offers a variety of housing. It is widely believed that having different kinds of housing will increase your chances of attracting martins.

systems. This is perhaps the most important aspect of housing from a management point of view, since easy access to each compartment is one of the keys to successful management.

Aluminum housing is available in a wide variety of sizes and styles and from many manufacturers. There are big differences in quality from one company to the other, so keep the important housing criteria in mind when you are shopping for an aluminum house. See box, page 23. The biggest manufacturers of aluminum houses are Nature House, Inc., and Coates Manufacturing, Inc. Between these two there are dozens of designs and models. In addition to houses, some companies offer important accessories like porch dividers, entrance hole plugs, and owl guards. See Resources, p. 92.

The disadvantages of aluminum housing include poor insulation and antiquated designs. As a building material, aluminum does not insulate very well; this means that housing can get dangerously hot during prolonged heat waves and dangerously cold during late springs. These are important considerations for landlords everywhere, but especially those at either temperature extreme of the martin breeding range.

Furthermore, manufacturers of aluminum houses have been slow to adopt recently discovered design innovations that have proven to be very beneficial to the birds. These include cavity entrances that repel starlings; deeper compartments to protect eggs, nestlings, and adults from many predators; offset entrance holes, which can greatly increase the occupancy rates; and elimination of porches and perches that may not be necessary and may actually tempt nestlings to leave the nest earlier than they should (which, in turn, makes them more likely to fall to the ground).

Wooden Houses

Wooden houses have been made for hundreds of years. The first multicompartment colonies were undoubtedly made of wood, and any housing that dates before the 1960s is usually made of wood. In the Victorian era, immense and elaborate Purple Martin houses were constructed.

One of the biggest advantages of wood is that it insulates better than other materials. This makes compartments cooler in hot weather and warmer in cool weather.

Another quality of wood is that you can build houses to more exact dimensions. The last few years of design research have revealed several important innovations that can increase the occupancy rates at colonies and also decrease chances of predation, thus making a safer and healthier environment for the martins. These innovations are easy to incorporate into designs made of wood.

The disadvantages of wood are that the houses can be very heavy and often take a lot of time, energy, and money to construct. Wooden houses also need to be maintained more than aluminum houses and require repair and repainting every few years. It is best to use oil-based white stain, rather than paint, for it does not peel and lasts longer.

The weight of wooden houses is a problem when putting them up and taking them down and when trying to lower them for monitoring. They are too heavy to lower on telescoping poles and so a winching system is needed to gain access to them once they are in use.

See Resources for manufacturers of wooden houses and ways to get plans to build your own.

Gourds Are Good

Natural Gourds — Gourds have been used longer than any other material as Purple Martin housing. The Native American tribes of the Southeast that attracted martins used hollowed-out calabash bottle gourds to accomplish their goals. These were hung from exposed branches and poles and were homes to the first martins that used artificial housing.

One of the big advantages of gourds is that they are inexpensive. Compared with aluminum or wooden houses, a small rack of gourds can be a money saver. If you like gardening and want to save

A conventional 12-compartment aluminum house. One of the advantages to this kind of housing is that it is light enough to be raised and lowered easily.

Two wooden houses. They offer deep compartments and offset cavity holes, lowering male porch-domination, a problem with more traditional designs.

even more on martin housing, you can grow your own gourds — the Purple Martin Conservation Association (see Resources) offers a handy pamphlet and sells gourd seeds.

Furthermore, gourds offer martins large nesting spaces. Most are 8–12 inches wide inside and very tall, so there is plenty of room for the nestlings. Even better, the swinging action of the gourds, which does not bother Purple Martins, tends to repel most nest-cavity competitors, such as starlings and House Sparrows, as well as predators.

The disadvantage of gourds is that, compared with wood and aluminum houses, they are not as durable. However, if properly cared for, they can usually last about ten years, and they are inexpensive to replace.

If you buy gourds, they need to be treated with a fungicide called copper sulfate, sanded, and then painted white. For management purposes, an access door should be added to the side or rear, so that you can easily get into the compartment to do nest checks (see page 86 for tips on how to do this).

Make sure the entrance holes in gourds are properly drilled. The hole should not face upward or it will let rain inside the gourd. Neither should the hole be too high above the bottom of the gourd, although this can be modified by adding nesting material, such as pine needles, so that the floor is about an inch below the bottom of the hole.

Plastic Gourds — Plastic gourds are now commercially available. They do not need to be treated and painted like natural gourds, and they come in connecting halves, making them easy to clean out at the end of the year. However, it is difficult to put access doors on the sides of plastic gourds, the inside compartment is smaller than in most natural gourds, and they are not as well insulated as natural gourds. In addition, the two halves may not seal tightly and may let water into the nest area.

Building Your Own

Building your own martin housing can be fun, for there is a lot of room for innovation and creativity. Many landlords find it especially satisfying to attract martins to housing that they built.

If you choose to design and build your own house, there are several factors to take into consideration. While there are certainly no rules about what the end product looks like — not every martin house has to look like a human house, in other words — you should create a space that is safe and healthy for the martins. Look at the list of good housing features in this chapter to be sure that your design offers the safest possible environment for Purple Martins. Remember that the housing must be practical for

A male looking out of a gourd. Gourds offer a number of advantages: they have large nest compartments, they repel some nest-site competitors and predators, and they are relatively inexpensive.

both birds and humans. Practicality is more important than looks.

Poles

Every martin colony needs a pole, and there are a number of things you should know about poles before you begin shopping. What you want to remember is that the best pole for *you* should allow you to safely and easily monitor the housing.

The three most widely used poles are telescoping poles, poles with a winch system, and poles with a pulley and rope. Telescoping poles are composed of a series of poles each smaller than the last, much like the segments of a collapsible telescope. You lower the house by taking out metal pins that hold the poles in place and carefully lowering each smaller pole. This works only for relatively light loads, like small aluminum houses, and therefore is incompatible with most wooden houses and colonies of many gourds. If telescoping poles are used, it is essential when raising the house to make sure the compartments face in exactly the same direction they faced before the house was lowered. Otherwise the birds may become confused and abandon the colony.

Poles with a more elaborate winch system have a cable that goes over a pulley at the top of the pole and attaches to the house. Through the use of a winch at the base of the pole you lower the house. A simplified version of this is a rope-and-pulley system, in which a rope attached to the top of the house goes over a pulley at the top of the pole and then attaches to a cleat near the bottom of the pole. Using this setup is like raising and lowering a flag. In both of these cases, the house actually has a hole through its center for the pole. Pulley systems can handle much heavier loads than telescoping poles do, so keep this in mind if you are planning on a heavy wooden or large aluminum house.

Avoid poles that pivot or tilt, unless you have gourds or a setup that will keep the house from tilting. Tipping a house on its side is very destructive and should never be done when martins are nesting inside, for the eggs or young can fall out, causing the failure of the colony and possible desertion of the site.

Predator Guards

All colonies should have predator guards on the poles. The objective of any pole guard is to keep predators from climbing the pole. You should consider owl guards as well, to deny owls access to the nest cavities. Even if you or others around you are sure there are no predators in your area, it is better to be safe. Most Purple Martin predators are nocturnal, so you would rarely see them, and all it takes is one serious attack by an owl or raccoon to cause colony abandonment by the martins. (See the chapter Dealing with Predators for more detail.)

Pole Baffles — A pole baffle can be an inverted metal cone 36–40 inches in diameter, a stovepipe around the pole, or some other commercially available baffle. These types of guards are highly effective obstacles to predators such as raccoons and can be effective against snakes in the South.

PVC Pipe — Putting 4–6 feet of 6-inch-diameter PVC pipe around the base of the pole makes the pole unclimbable by most predators, including snakes.

What Does *Not* Work — Smearing petroleum jelly, axle grease, or other, similar substances around the pole rarely deters snakes or raccoons, so do not rely

What to Look For in Good Martin Houses

1. Housing should be easy to raise and lower vertically (that is, without tilting the house) for monitoring and cleaning.

2. Each cavity should be easily accessible for monitoring and cleaning. A door for each nest compartment is best, or one large door for every floor side.

3. Entrance holes should be 2 inches in diameter, and 1 inch above the floor of the cavity. Martins will accept any diameter between 1 3/4 and 2 1/2 inches.

4. Cavities should measure at least 6 inches wide, 6 inches high, and 9–12 inches deep. Larger compartments are better, but may attract starlings.

5. Housing should have a white exterior. Trim can be any color.

6. Housing should be well ventilated.

7. Housing should keep compartments dry and drain out any water that might get in. Slightly raised subfloors can be used in nest compartments to keep nests dry.

8. Housing materials should insulate the birds from heat and cold.

9. Housing does *not* need to have perches or railings.

10. Housing should not be able to turn in wind. Housing that turns (i.e., that does not consistently face in exactly the same direction) may disorient the birds and result in colony abandonment. The swinging action of gourds is accepted by martins, but gourds also should not be able to turn.

The house on the left has "the works" — gourds, extra perches, owl guards, and good pole guards. The cylindrical object hanging below the house is a radio transmitter that allows the landlord to hear the sounds of the colony from inside his or her home.

be bought or homemade. For more on owl guards and protection from owls, see Dealing with Predators, page 70.

In the end, what you want to achieve is an adequate housing system that raises and lowers easily and prevents predators from reaching the cavities. In addition to an adequate habitat, these qualities are what it takes to create a good colony.

on this strategy alone. It usually just results in a messy predator.

Owl Guards — These are vertical bars placed across the front of the Purple Martin housing to prevent owls from reaching in and getting the birds. They can

Spring Arrival

Spring Is Here

For thousands of landlords across the country, the return of Purple Martins is the first sign of spring. The calls and song of their beloved birds bring back the excitement and enjoyment of being a landlord and are the prelude to an active breeding season that will go on for the next several months.

Purple Martins are indeed some of the first migrants to return to North America in spring, and there is speculation that for the first people who attracted them, the birds' arrival marked the beginning of the growing season and the time to plant their crops.

Migration Mysteries

Each spring Purple Martins make a long migration to their breeding grounds in North America. They come from South America — mostly Brazil — and travel over huge expanses of land and water. Martins going all the way to central Canada travel up to 7,000 miles. It is assumed that martins take about two months to make the trip.

There are still many mysteries to the migration of Purple Martins. It is unknown, for instance, how long it really takes an individual bird to fly from its wintering site to its breeding site, or whether this trip is continuous or broken into several shorter

Martin descending from the skies to housing. This is a happy sight for landlords attracting martins for the first time.

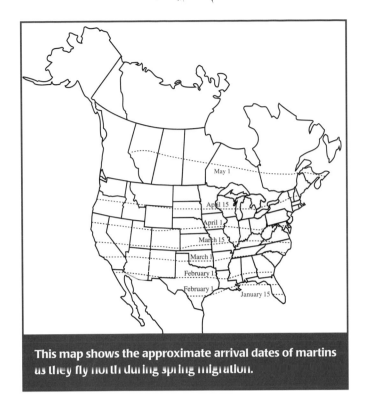

This map shows the approximate arrival dates of martins as they fly north during spring migration.

stretches. Do they fly all day? At what speeds? Do they fly at night? The answers to these questions are also unknown.

Another unknown of the migration is what route the birds take. It is generally assumed that once martins reach the northern part of South America, they take one of three routes to the United States and Canada. One of these would be over land, funneling through Central America and then continuing over Mexico. Another route may cross the Gulf of Mexico, probably between the Yucatan Peninsula, in Mexico, and the Mississippi Delta, in Louisiana. The third major route may utilize the islands of the Caribbean, the Greater Antilles, and the peninsula of Florida, and is referred to as the island-hopping route. It is unclear which of these routes is used most.

Whatever routes the birds use, however, the migration is strenuous. Many are too weak to make the entire trip and die along the way. Thus, their arrival in your backyard marks the end of an incredible journey, one that brings martins thousands of miles, from one hemisphere to another.

When and Where to Expect Whom

Look for returning martins in your area according to the accompanying migration map above. This map, generated by the arrival dates recorded by colony landlords, illustrates the average time of year the first adult birds return to different areas as they gradually make their way north. These are martins that have successfully bred before and are returning to established sites.

Second-year martins, called subadults, will start returning 4–6 weeks later than the adults. This is important to know if you are trying to attract martins for the first time, for these young birds are the primary individuals that will come to unestablished sites and colonize them. (Sometimes adult males who have lost their sites come and start new colonies.) Most subadult martins return to the general area where they were born.

Some Risks of Early Arrival

The spring migration of Purple Martins is determined by the availability of flying insects, which in turn is determined by the temperature. Thus, another way to look at the migration map is as a record of the gradual northward movement of warm temperatures that are able to sustain populations of flying insects.

Although it is nice to have Purple Martins be among the first migrants to return, this early arrival is sometimes difficult for the birds. Returning as early as they do, and being completely dependent on flying insects, Purple Martins can suffer during unseasonably cold or wet springs. These conditions keep insects from flying and, as a result, martins may die from starvation. Refer to the chapter Adverse Weather and Martins, page 80, to find actions you can take during bad weather that will increase the chances of survival for the martins at your colony.

If it is risky, why do Purple Martins return so early? The answer is reproductive success. The sooner an individual returns to a specific site and selects a compartment or group of compartments to defend, the better chance it has of successfully attracting a mate, breeding, and creating many offspring.

It is also possible that martins, over the last century, have started returning earlier in response to competition from introduced species like House Sparrows and European Starlings.

What Are "Scouts"?

Many people think that the earliest returning martins scout out prospective colony sites and then return for other martins in order to guide them to the colony.

This is not true. While it may be true that early-arriving martins explore a variety of sites, most birds either stay at the site once they arrive or stay briefly and then move on to their final site. In any case, they do not backtrack or go south to help other Purple Martins coming north.

There are two good reasons why this notion of scouts is not true for Purple Martins. First, birds have superb orientation capabilities and do not need to be guided back to nesting areas. Purple Martins, in fact, will often return to the same compartment year after year. Sometimes martins returning to established sites where the housing has not yet been put up for the season will hover in the air exactly where the colony was the previous season.

Second, the early birds are back for the proverbial worm. Those that return first often establish themselves at the most desirable compartments and sites, thus increasing their chances of finding a mate and breeding successfully.

If you ever observe martins coming to your colony, especially at unestablished sites, and then leaving after a few days, they are probably on their way to another location and simply resting at your site. Or they may have to leave temporarily due to lack of food and will return when there are more insects to eat.

Martins are some of the most graceful fliers in the bird family, and many landlords enjoy sitting back and just watching them glide through the air.

This male arrived early in the season to get the best choice of nest holes. The notion that there are "scouts" who arrive early and then go back to get the rest of the colony is untrue.

What and How Do Purple Martins Eat?

How Purple Martins Feed

Like most members of the swallow family, Purple Martins eat only insects. In fact, they pretty much eat only flying insects, for all of their feeding is done on the wing.

As they feed, martins stay in loose aerial groups, flying through the air in pursuit of food, alternatively taking deep flaps and then gliding for a while, often in circles or shallow arcs.

It is usually very difficult to actually see Purple Martins catch their prey, but once in a while you will see a martin gliding smoothly along and then suddenly make an abrupt direction change or quick drop; this is a bird going after an insect.

Martins typically forage a few hundred feet in the air, sometimes as high as 500 feet. However, it is not uncommon to see a martin swoop down from a perch at the colony to catch an insect passing below.

Purple Martins prefer to forage in open areas where there are plenty of insects and lots of room to hunt. Areas such as pastures, farmland, the edges of forests, and open water — especially over insect-rich wetlands — tend to be the best places to look for foraging martins. Sometimes a colony will be near a feeding area, but it is not unusual for martins, at least in spring and before breeding, to fly a few miles in search of food. Large insect populations occur in varying areas over the course of the summer, so the birds often have to search out new locations in which to find prey.

The Menu

The diet of Purple Martins, although composed mostly of flying insects, changes over the course of the breeding season. For instance, studies show that for the first two months after arrival as much as two-thirds of their diet comes from one family of insects — Hymenoptera (bees, ants, and wasps) — but that later in the season the majority of their food comes from other insect families, which become more numerous as the summer wears on.

Insects that Purple Martins frequently eat include flies, beetles, moths, butterflies, dragonflies, grasshoppers, hemipteran bugs, hoverflies, spiders, and mayflies. Other food includes wasps, stink bugs, treehoppers, some caterpillars, and even cicadas. While almost all of their food is caught in the air, Purple Martins have been observed eating insects off the ground, usually ants.

A female with a dragonfly in her mouth. This is a common sight when parents are feeding their young.

Martins are incredibly adept at catching flying insects. Most of their hunting occurs several hundred feet in the air.

In addition to these natural foods, martins will come to certain feeders where there are crushed eggshells, which they use as a source of grit and calcium. With some work, they can also be "trained" to eat mealworms placed on feeders (see page 64).

What About Mosquitoes?

Contrary to popular belief, Purple Martins do not eat huge numbers of mosquitoes. In fact, scientific studies reveal that mosquitoes compose, at most, 3 percent of the diet of Purple Martins.

There are a few simple reasons why Purple Martins do not eat large numbers of mosquitoes. First, they usually eat insects that are larger than mosquitoes. Second, martins feed at very high elevations, sometimes up to 500 feet, where mosquitoes are rarely found; mosquitoes tend to stick close to the ground and are usually in heavy vegetation. Third, mosquitoes are most active right around dusk and later. At this time of day, Purple Martins stop feeding and are retiring for the night.

Mosquitoes, then, will go on living in the presence of martin colonies, even though it is widely believed that they are the staple of the Purple Martin diet.

Food for the Young

When providing food for nestlings, adult martins will catch anywhere from a few to hundreds of insects at a time, compressing them in their mouth into a tight ball called a bolus. These collected insects are held pressed to the roof of the bird's mouth by its tongue as the bird continues to collect more insects. The difference in number of insects collected in one trip usually depends on how far away the bird has to go for food — the greater the distance traveled, the larger the bolus. These packed meals are brought back to the nest compartment and fed to the nestlings.

As the nestlings get bigger, adults will start bringing much larger insects, such as dragonflies, damselflies, and butterflies. Despite the large size of these insects relative to the nestlings, they are eaten whole, not broken into bite-sized chunks. This is an interesting time for the observer who can watch as food is visibly passed from the parents to the open mouths of nestlings.

Territory and Courtship

Behavior to Watch

Purple Martins are fun to watch because all of their breeding behavior takes place on or near the colony. The constant activity around a colony may appear to be chaotic, but in fact it has structure and meaning. Having a working knowledge of the social behavior of Purple Martins will enable you to observe, understand, and increasingly enjoy the fast-paced life of the birds at your colony.

The first part of the breeding season is the most socially active, as the martins arrive, stake out and defend territories, and form breeding pairs through courtship. As the season wears on, this social activity wanes, for the birds become invested in the development of their young. Thus, the first couple of months offer some exciting behavior-watching. Colonies are most active early in the morning, when all of the birds are there.

Arriving and Establishing Territories

Males and females return to the colony at approximately the same time. It may seem as if the males come first, but this is only because the first item on their agenda is to establish and advertise a territory, making them very vocal and visible to the observer.

When defining a territory, a male repeatedly goes in and out of nest compartments, finally choosing one or several cavities to defend from other males. Thus, his territory consists of the nest holes and the immediate area in front of them. There have been a few cases when a male has tried to defend an entire house from other males, but this is rare.

In gourds and houses that have greater spacing between compartments, males usually defend only one nesting compartment each.

Territory Defense

Males proclaim their possession of a territory by singing. This is usually done from the cavity, from a nearby perch, from the porch outside the cavity, or from the roof of the house (even though the roof is a neutral space and is never defended). The singing intensifies as other males come near and especially if

A pair of martins at a gourd. Both members of the pair will defend a breeding territory, but the male is usually more aggressive and defends a larger area than the female.

A pair of Purple Martins perching on a snag.

an intruder enters the territory. If the intruder is persistent, fights may occur, sometimes becoming quite violent.

It is not uncommon to see two males, feet locked in midair, fall to the ground in a heated battle. During these fights they give frequent "hee-hee" calls and sometimes peck at each other repeatedly. Fighting males have the ability to inflict serious harm to each other, and sometimes males will be killed as the result of these territorial skirmishes. More often, however, the fight is brief and ends with the martins flying back to the house. The victor, which is usually the defender, will sing from his territory, and the loser may assume the stooped-submissive posture (see the chapter Purple Martin Language).

Territories are defended most diligently in the morning and again at dusk — times when the social activity of the colony is high. Once territories become

established, however, there is little fighting. In fact, at this time, a martin may defend his neighbor's territory from an intruder when that neighbor is away, possibly to preserve the status quo in the area of his own nest hole. This usually happens a few days after the colony is settled.

After pairs form, the female will also defend the territory, often only from other females. Females usually defend only one nest hole.

Over the course of the breeding season, male territorial defense wanes and males stop defending extra compartments that they are not using. This is a natural result of pairs putting more energy into nest building and raising the young.

It has been suggested that the defense of several nest holes by males may increase their opportunities to be polygynous (mate with more than one female). Studies reveal that polygyny is attempted by about

20 percent of males at a colony but only successfully accomplished by about 5 percent. Some polygynous males help raise at least two different broods. Others may stop helping one of their mates somewhere along the line. The abandoned females often get help feeding their young from other males, usually unpaired males, called floaters (see later in this chapter).

Because the design of conventional martin houses makes the defense of more than one nesting compartment very easy for the males, occupancy rates are often half of what they could be. This is why colonies of gourds and other single-unit housing, or houses that are designed with plenty of space between cavity entrances, often have a higher occupancy rate. Porch dividers are available for some conventional housing; when there are physical barriers between nesting compartments, individual males tend to defend fewer cavities, and thus more cavities are made available to breeding pairs.

Territory Advertising

Males defend their territories and then advertise themselves and the accompanying compartment or group of compartments to females. This is done through a number of displays, most notably the claiming-reclaiming display (see next chapter) and singing. Males will sing loudly from their territories, sometimes while sticking their heads out of a nest hole. They may also repeatedly enter and exit nest holes as fast as they can. These behaviors are intensified in the presence of females and are thought to be an attempt at attracting females to the territory.

Females control the formation of pairs, for they are the ones who pick a mate and his territory. Females can be aggressive toward each other when deciding on mates. For instance, if a female is inspecting a territory and another female comes by, the first one will chase the second away, even if she has not yet decided whether she will stay there.

Pair Formation

Pairs are formed a few hours to a few days after the arrival of both males and females at a colony. There is no display that clearly marks the moment a pair forms; rather, over time a male and a female

This female and male martin look comfortably paired. A pair may take several days to develop a strong bond.

A male singing from a nest hole with a female hovering in front. Males singing to females from within nest holes is a common behavior during courtship.

simply start acting like a pair — loafing, preening, foraging, and, most important, defending their territory together. At this time, they also start to greet each other with singing or cher-calls, especially after having been apart.

Pair behavior is most often seen in the mornings, when Purple Martin activity is at its highest, and then again at night.

Floaters

At every colony, there will always be a few birds that do not breed that season. These are usually subadult males, and are referred to as floaters by researchers. Floaters participate in several types of behavior.

If you ever see a nestling wander onto a porch area and then quickly get knocked to the ground by an older bird, it is usually a floater that is responsible. Most researchers think these birds are trying to make a pair's breeding attempt unsuccessful, which in turn

may dissolve their bond and free up a female with which the floater could then mate.

A second easily recognized activity of floaters is the incessant harassment of fledglings. From the time fledglings first leave the nest until they are old enough to start feeding on their own, floaters are always lurking around perches and the housing to harass them.

Floaters may repeatedly peck at these fledglings while the young martins are flying between the colony and a spot where they spend the day and get fed by their parents. Researchers think that this kind of immediate harassment keeps the young from imprinting on that site and returning to it to breed the following season, thus reducing the competition for the floaters in the next year.

Purple Martin Language

What's All That Squawking and Fighting About?

Purple Martins use a language of sounds and physical postures to communicate with each other and coordinate their lives. These are called vocal and visual displays. Some of the displays you might hear or see at your colony have very specific meanings, while others can be given in a wide range of contexts and mean a number of different things. Knowing about the language of Purple Martins can help you understand more of the complex social activity at your colony.

Vocal Displays

Despite the array of sounds Purple Martins make, there are only a few that you will hear regularly. This section will list the most common sounds and explain the contexts in which they are given. The term *song* refers to a long, often complex series of different sounds. Calls, on the other hand, are usually short, simple, one- or two-syllable sounds.

Song — The Purple Martin song is a series of paired notes, producing a gurgling, liquid phrase, and is from 2 to 6 seconds long.

Despite the complexity of sound around a colony, there are a few easily recognized calls and songs that you can pick out.

Song may be given in flight or at rest and under these circumstances: during the establishment of territory; when the male advertises himself and his territory to prospective females; when a pair rejoins after having been separated; when one bird replaces the other on the nest; during forced extra-pair copulations; and before or after copulation, or any other male-female interactions.

There are subtle differences between the songs of males and females, although song is used by both sexes in similar contexts.

The male song, often referred to as the croak-song, has a short grating sound at the very end of it. He also opens his bill widely to produce this grating sound, making it possible to visually identify which bird is actually singing. The female song, often called the chortle-song, does not have this ending and is a little muffled compared to the male version.

Dawnsong — This vocalization is given by males in the early predawn and dawn hours of the day. It is given hundreds of feet in the air as the males fly slowly over their colony site. Dawnsong is believed to help attract subadult martins to that particular colony site – which is why playing a recorded version of this song is a great strategy for attracting martins. The excellent acoustics of predawn — no wind and much moisture in the air — allow this song to travel for many miles. Dawnsong is discontinued after the migrating subadults have finished passing through a given area.

Cher-Call — This is a single- or double-syllable call sounding much like the written "cher" or "cher-cher."

Used by both males and females, this is by far the most common and widely used vocalization of Purple Martins at their breeding colonies. It is given in almost any context, can be interspersed with other calls or song, and is often accompanied by quick flips and shakes of the wings or body.

Some of the more common contexts for this call: as birds approach the colony; as perched birds are greeted by their neighbors; from one bird to its mate; during courtship; for mild alarm; or simply while perched at the colony site. It is believed that this call might be individually distinct and act as a kind of personal identification of each bird.

Zweet-Call — This is a short, one-syllable call with

A male martin calling from a porch. The wide-open bill is a telltale sign of the grating sound produced at the end of the male's version of song.

a definite "eee" sound that sometimes descends slightly at the end, resulting in "zweert."

It has two general meanings. The first is as a high-intensity alarm, given in flight as the martins fly from the housing, circle overhead, or perch above a predator on the ground. Other kinds of birds, especially predatory ones, other animals, and people will often cause the martins to become alarmed. Purple Martins will give zweet-calls when you approach their colony, especially if they have had limited exposure to people at such close quarters.

The second context of the zweet-call is when a new arrival is spotted at the colony, especially if it is a female, or if a male spots another male near his mate. Males chasing other males who are trying to engage in forced extra-pair copulations will also give this call.

The interesting thing about the zweet-call is that the general population of birds at a colony can easily and quickly differentiate between its two meanings. For instance, the birds will not scatter if a male gives this call when he spots another male near his mate, but they become alert if it is given in response to a cat or other potential predator spotted on the ground nearby.

Hee-Hee-Call — This call is a series of 4–10 hoarse, high-pitched sounds much like "hee-hee-hee." It is given at the rate of about four "hee's" per second.

This call is not very common and is given mostly by males in territorial disputes, including the aggressive fights in which they fall to the ground. After returning to the housing, participants in the fighting may each give this call from their respective territories. This call occasionally accompanies the claiming-reclaiming display (see below).

It is unclear whether females give this call, for they are usually silent when defending their territory from other females.

Juvenile-Call — This is a single short, harsh call given about 2–3 times per second. It is the first consistent vocalization that Purple Martin nestlings make, starting at around 24 days of age. While still in the nest, the young will make this call whenever a parent or other adult bird approaches the cavity opening. It is also given after the young fledge, especially when the birds are moving to the grouping areas, are in danger, or as parents arrive at the assembled broods with food. Juveniles are otherwise silent, even when zweet-calls are given by the adults.

Visual Displays

Several visual displays are used by martins. These are distinctive actions or postures; some of them have very specific meanings, while others are used in a number of different situations. Most of them are accompanied by vocalizations. What follows is an overview of the most common visual displays and what they mean.

Claiming-Reclaiming Display — This display is accompanied by song and involves the male leaving a nest hole, flying in a large circle, and returning to the hole in a steep dive punctuated with fluttering wings as he lands. He then quickly enters the hole, turns around, and sings from this position. It is done most frequently when male martins are trying to attract females to their territories.

Horizontal Threat Display — In this display the body of the bird is horizontal and the feathers on the crest may be slightly raised. Gaping and bill-snapping may accompany this posture.

This is an aggressive display used by both sexes when they are threatening a nearby bird, whether another martin or a nest-site competitor like a House Sparrow or European Starling. It is most often used by males during territorial squabbles.

Martins give calls under all kinds of circumstances, ranging from the greeting of mates to harsh warning calls when predators are near.

An adult pair of Purple Martins taking a break from their otherwise constant activity.

Gaping — This is a display in which one bird opens its bill widely at another bird. It is sometimes accompanied by slight lunges, and often precipitates aggressive fighting. It is used by both sexes in interactions with nest-site competitors and in mild interaction between mates.

Bill-Snapping — In this display the bill is forcibly snapped shut, making a sound that can be heard over the general chatter of the colony. Like gaping, this action is often intermingled with other aggressive displays or postures. It is less common than gaping, but seems to indicate the same aggressive intention. It is also used toward other species of birds.

Feather Maintenance

Several other actions that martins do throughout the breeding cycle are worth mentioning, most of them revolving around the maintenance of feathers. Although these may at times look like displays, they are not part of language.

Preening and Stretching — Birds clean their feathers by preening. They do this by scratching parts of their body with their feet, especially the head, and also running their bill along chest, wing, and tail feathers. This action helps keep their feathers free of dust and dirt, as well as parasites. Preening is often combined with stretching of wings and is most commonly done in the late afternoon.

Sunning — Sunning is important for martins because it helps maintain the health of their feathers by stimulating the production of vitamin D and by causing parasites to move to places where the bird can remove them. You might look out at the colony one day and see all the martins assuming bizarre postures at their perches. These postures vary from simply tilting a head toward the sky to practically lying down with bill open and tongue outstretched. Sunning birds keep their eyes open, often when looking straight up into the bright sun, and may be motionless for several minutes if left undisturbed.

Bathing and Drinking — Martins bathe and drink on the wing, flying low over water in loose groups or by themselves, quickly dipping their tails into the water and then rising up into the air. Sometimes they just dip their bills into the water for a quick sip. Bathing is often followed by preening.

Nest Building

Watching Nest Building

Nest building begins about 4–6 weeks after the first birds arrive at the colony and continues for 3–4 weeks. Males start nest building, but the females end up doing most of the work. A shallow nest of twigs, grasses, and mud is the standard Purple Martin nest, but there are all kinds of variations to this theme.

Nest building is a casual affair for martins, but it brings with it a host of behaviors and activities for landlords to enjoy. Watching martins gather nest material is a special treat and can help you follow the progress of your breeding pairs.

There are several things you can do as a landlord to help your martins, such as supplying extra nesting material and creating mud puddles. A section later in this chapter will give you tips on how to do this.

The Beginning of Construction

The first signs of nest building are males flying to the ground, picking up pieces of nest material, drop-

A male martin inspecting a gourd as a potential breeding cavity. It is common to see males going in and out of cavities as they try to establish territories.

A female (left) sunning on the porch. Activities such as this and preening often indicate a calm and comfortable atmosphere at the colony.

ping them, and then flying away. In successive attempts, the males might bring the material halfway to the box, only to drop it in midair, or all the way there, but not succeed in getting it through the nesting hole. Their attempts seem halfhearted, for they rarely gather significant amounts of material for the actual construction of the nest.

This can go on for a couple of days before the females start to join in. Females gather nesting material and actually get it into the nesting compartment. After a while, males slow down in their efforts and the females take over, eventually building the nest mostly by themselves.

If a martin has trouble getting material into one compartment, or that opening is being blocked by their mate, they will often carry it to another compartment within their territory. Thus, it is not uncommon to find half-built nests in a number of compartments, even if they are not being used.

Nest building continues as the main activity of the pair for a few days but then stops for a week or two. When it starts up again, it is less intense and usually only done in the mornings.

Nest building has been referred to as a contagious activity at Purple Martin colonies, for as soon as one pair starts to do it, everybody else seems to catch the spirit and join in. It is not uncommon to see one pair engaged in the collection of material on one morning and then see several pairs doing it the next morning. The pace of construction varies from pair to pair, and especially from age group to age group. Subadult pairs, who are breeding for the first time and who arrive at the colony much later, usually do not take as long to build their nest.

Nest Materials

Materials used in the construction vary widely. Most martin nests are made of twigs, straw, and mud, although all kinds of things have turned up, including glass, gum wrappers, matchbooks, plastic tabs from take-out coffee lids, and even a diamond.

The bed of the nest is usually only about 1 inch deep, but this dimension can vary between a scattering of twigs on the floor of the cavity to a well-made platform. A slight depression may be in the center or toward the rear of the cavity, and there can be a mud wall just inside the nest hole.

The use of mud varies widely from location to location, even from nest to nest. It also varies according to the moisture conditions of each season and proximity of the colony to mud. Some nest holes

This female has gathered a twig and perched near her mate before taking the twig to the nest.

kinds of trees and shrubs are subjected to this gathering, martins seem to have their favorite leaves, including apple, pear, willow, elm, cherry, maple, aspen, and oak.

Leaf gathering is started during the egg-laying period and continues through the incubation period. The leaves eventually dry up and remain in the nest.

It is still unknown what function these leaves serve, but most people speculate that they emit tiny amounts of a chemical called hydrocyanic acid, a kind of natural insecticide that might protect the nestlings or incubating female from certain parasites. People also believe that the leaves might add moisture to the nest and help regulate the temperature inside the cavity. Others suggest that the gathering might be a behavioral display, since it is so closely tied with copulation and egg laying. It is also possible that the leaves help hide the eggs and protect them from predators when the parents are away.

The neatness of a nest varies widely. Some constructions are barely discernible from a pile of twigs; others are highly crafted platforms with a gently

have so much mud in them, one wonders how the birds can get in and out, while others have only a trace amount or none at all. Houses with larger openings tend to have more mud. It is widely believed that the mud, which always forms a slight wall immediately inside the hole and gradually slopes back toward the rear of the compartment, acts as a guard against foul weather and predators, and protects the eggs.

There are occasionally unusual nests, some of which are made out of anything but natural materials, including steel nails, cat or dog hair, and tinfoil.

Completion and Green Leaf Gathering

Toward the completion of the nest and continuing until the eggs hatch, green leaves are gathered by the pair and used to line the cup of the nest. Leaf-seeking martins — usually males, although females do it too — land in nearby greenery and tear off leaves with their bills. This is an easy activity to spot, for the birds flail about in their efforts to grab leaves. While all

A male bringing a green leaf to his nest. Leaves are gathered mostly by the males, during the egg-laying and incubation periods.

If you see a martin in a bush, it is probably gathering green leaves for its nest, as this one is.

sloping bowl protected by a mud wall. More often than not, it is older birds that have more crafted nests, but this is not always the case.

The nest disintegrates as the season wears on and the young grow. If nest replacements are not done, what is left at the end of the season after the young fledge bears little resemblance to a cohesive nest. Rather, it looks more like a scattering of twigs, dried leaves, and crumbled mud.

Tips for Landlords

There are a few things landlords can do to make this period easier for the martins. Supplying building pairs with artificial nesting material can be helpful to the birds. Purple Martins will use a wide variety of material to build nests.

Many people put out cut pieces of straw or grass. If you choose to do this, cut the pieces in 4–6-inch lengths and make sure that the clippings are dry. Try to keep these offerings away from shrubbery or other concealing vegetation, where a cat or other predator may be hiding.

You can also create additional mud for the martins by watering areas of exposed soil. Using a bucket or hose, simply wet these areas so that they become muddy.

Other Behavior During Nest Building

Copulation — Just before and during egg laying, copulation occurs. This is rarely seen done by mated pairs and it is believed that they mate inside the nest compartment. Part of the reason for this may be because mating outside the nest attracts other males, who may interfere and try to force mating with the female.

Females may be able to lay a clutch of eggs from one copulation. Each egg is produced by the female within a 24-hour period. Occasionally eggs are laid that are infertile and will not hatch.

Extra-Pair Copulations — During nest building, especially toward the end of this period, right before egg laying, both adult and subadult females are chased by groups of 4–6 adult male martins, none of whom are her mate, who try to copulate with the female. This most commonly happens when females

Opened compartments in an aluminum house. Note the mud wall in the middle compartment. The pine needles have been provided by the landlord as artificial nesting material.

Many landlords provide the martins at their colonies with artificial nesting material. The basket contains pieces of straw for the birds to use. The metal platter contains crushed eggshells, which the martins eat for grit and calcium.

are on or near the ground gathering nesting material and after a lone male flies to her and tries to copulate. This seems to send a signal to other males, who then join in chasing the female. These are called forced extra-pair copulations.

More often than not, this occurs to females paired to subadult males. If there is a male escorting her every move — a behavior called mate-guarding — the attack is usually thwarted. If the first attacker is driven off by a male mate-guarding a female, then the contagious nature of the activity ceases. If a female is not accompanied by her mate and is approached by a group of males, her mate will quickly come to her aid and try to keep away the approaching males. Adult males typically mate-guard their mates more frequently than subadult males.

Why does this happen? There are different theories about the reason for this activity, but recent research suggests it may be connected with eastern martins' adoption of colonial life.

Why, for instance, have Purple Martins become colonial nesters? Colonial nesting behavior makes large demands on birds, demands that solitary nesting birds do not have to deal with, like intraspecific competition, increases in parasites and disease transmission, and competition for resources.

One of the reasons this may have developed is the opportunity for extra-pair copulation. Adult males

A group of males at a colony. Extra-pair copulations usually start when a male or group of males spots a female on the ground as she collects nesting material.

who engage in extra-pair copulations and the females who lay those eggs *both* benefit. The males are able to spread their genes and the females have clutches that are genetically diverse. In the long run, having such a brood will be beneficial. For example, perhaps a certain nestling has genes that make it slightly more tolerant of parasites than its nest-mates, helping it survive a period of heavy infesta-tion.

Pair Chase — There is another kind of activity that involves males chasing females during this period, but it is done by only one male toward his own mate. This is called pair chase. Unlike extra-pair copula-tions, pair chase happens away from the colony and at significant heights in the air. It usually happens as a pair are foraging together. The male will suddenly begin to chase his mate, singing loudly. The chase can stop almost immediately or carry on for 15–40 sec-onds. During the chase, the female tries all kinds of evasive maneuvers to lose her mate, sometimes coming close to the ground. The chase stops as sud-denly as it starts, and the pair resume foraging together. Its function is unknown.

An adult female perched above a gourd. During nest building, females may copulate with males other than their mates. This usually occurs after several males have chased her.

Egg Laying and Incubation

All Quiet on the Home Front

The whole egg-laying and incubation period at the colony is a relatively quiet time. The only noticeable behavior going on is the gathering of green leaves, done mostly by the males.

However, this is an important time for a landlord, because this is the time to start monitoring. Each nest's clutch initiation date — the date when the first egg is laid — is important to know, for you can then calculate when the young in the nest will most likely fledge.

A pair at their gourd. The egg-laying and incubation periods are the quietest at the colony.

Egg Laying

Purple Martin adult females typically lay 5–7 pure white eggs; the average number is 5. Subadult females lay 3–5 eggs. The female lays 1 egg early in the morning on each of several successive days. This activity begins within a week after completing the nest and about 2 months after the first martins arrive at the colony.

When they are first laid, the eggs have a slight sheen on them, but afterward they are a dull white color. Eggs are typically a little less than 1 1/8 inches long and a little less than 3/4 inch wide. Each weighs approximately 4 grams (slightly under a tenth of an ounce).

Although the female usually lays 1 egg each day, if there is a cold spell, she may interrupt her laying for a day or two. If a clutch is destroyed or the young killed and this occurs early in the season, a second brood attempt may be made. These clutches usually consist of only 4 eggs. In other cases, if predation occurs, the adults may leave the site and not renest.

During adverse weather, when the birds are under stress from lack of food, clutches may be reduced to 2 or even just 1 egg. At the other extreme, there have been clutches of 9 eggs in one nest, and this is probably the result of two females laying eggs in the same compartment. Nobody knows for sure why this occurs.

Incubation

Incubation involves applying body heat to the eggs; in Purple Martins it is done by the female. It starts on the day the next to last egg is laid and continues for 14–16 days. The eggs that were first laid may undergo some development prior to the start of incubation. This may be because both adults sleep on the eggs and spend a lot of time in the compartment, thus elevating the temperature in the cavity and perhaps causing some development of the embryos. Therefore, the young of a single clutch may hatch all on the same day or over a period of 48 hours.

Incubation requires the active transfer of heat from the female's body to the outside of the egg. This is done through the brood patch, a featherless, bald area of skin on the belly of female Purple Martins. The feathers covering the brood patch are molted on breeding females just before egg laying begins, as the result of the release of hormones. This molting, coupled with the increase in size and number of blood vessels in this area, creates the brood patch. Brood patches are not visible to the observer, for they are covered by adjoining flank feathers. Brood patches disappear after incubation ends.

The female exposes her brood patch to the eggs by spreading her flank feathers, then settling onto the eggs. The eggs are periodically rotated, so that each part of the egg is incubated equally.

The male will spend a lot of time in the nest cavity and even on the nest during this period, but he is not actively incubating. Rather, the male will insulate the eggs, preventing heat or moisture loss while the female is away, an activity that is particularly important on cold days. Male martins cannot incubate because they do not develop brood patches.

Time Well Spent

The female spends, on average, about 70 percent of the day on the eggs. On colder days, she may spend as much as 90 percent of the day on the nest, but in hot weather, will spend significantly less time there.

Periods of incubation average 4–15 minutes long, but can be as short as 1 minute or as long as 35 minutes. These are interrupted by 5–10-minute breaks during which the female most often leaves to feed.

It is uncommon for male martins to provide food for their incubating mates. While the female is gone, her mate may enter the cavity and sit on the nest, enter the cavity and guard the entrance, or simply wait on the porch for her to return. These exchanges are usually started by the male coming to the entrance and singing to his mate.

Incubation requires a lot of energy from the female. If there is a sustained spell of cold weather during incubation and parents have to spend long periods looking for food, the parents might abandon

A typical Purple Martin nest, with a lining of green leaves and 5 white eggs. This landlord has also provided pine shavings for additional nest material.

their efforts to incubate the eggs in order to save themselves.

In periods of extremely hot weather, martins will make attempts to cool off the eggs. This is sometimes accomplished by wetting the feathers and wetting the eggs or by decreasing the amount of time spent on the eggs.

The female continues to sit over the nestlings even after they have hatched. This is called brooding, and it helps keep the young warm until they develop feathers. Brooding may continue for 2 weeks, by which time the young have feathers and can at least partially regulate their own body temperature.

Nestling Phase

Growing Up in the Nest

The time from when the eggs hatch to when the young leave the nest is called the nestling phase. This phase for martins lasts 25–30 days, with 28 days being the average. The nestling phase is a period of tremendous growth for the young martins and is marked by high levels of activity by the parents. Not only do the parents have to find food for themselves, but now they have several other mouths to feed.

Not all pairs at your colony will be doing the same things at the same times, especially when there are breeding pairs of subadult martins, who arrived and started to breed later than the adults. While one pair might be in the midst of feeding five healthy nestlings, their neighbors might just have begun to lay eggs.

After the young reach adult size and are fully developed, they will leave the nest — a process called fledging — and embark on their first flights, thus ending the nestling phase.

Hatching at Different Times

The eggs in a Purple Martin nest usually hatch over the course of 2 and sometimes 3 days. Occasionally all of the eggs in a nest will hatch on the same day.

It is important for landlords to know that in any given nest, there may be differences in age and development between the oldest and the youngest birds. Sometimes the difference is very slight, while other times it is easy to recognize.

This phenomenon of eggs hatching over several days is called asynchronous hatching. It is thought to actually increase the number of birds that successfully leave the nest. For instance, during a good breeding season with warm weather, low parasite

infestations, and no predation, all the young will survive and there will be a naturally higher success rate. During seasons with periods of bad weather or heavy parasite populations, however, there will be a lower success rate in nests. But because of asynchronous hatching, some of the young are older, more developed, and have a better chance of surviving these periods. If the nestlings were all the same age, severe weather or other problems might wipe them all out.

Nestlings grow at a fantastic rate, weighing about 2.75 grams at hatching, but doubling that within 1 day. Growth and development continue at a rapid pace until the young birds are about 15 days old. At 20 days they are at their peak weight and usually weigh several grams more than their parents (average weight 56 grams — about 2 ounces).

While nestlings are very young, one parent tends to stay at the nest while the other goes out to get food. When the foraging parent returns, they switch places. As the nestlings get older, both parents have to leave the nest and forage to meet their demands for food.

Recognizing Nestling Ages

The following descriptions of nestlings are based on their general appearance at different ages. Because individual young develop at varying rates, this will only enable you to make educated guesses about the ages of individual birds.

It is important to be able to tell the ages of nestlings, though, for if you find a nestling that has fallen from the nest and do not know which nest it came from, you can at least make sure to put it in a nest with nestlings of about the same age. If placed in a nest where it is older and stronger than its new siblings, it may keep those siblings from eating by taking all the food the parents bring to the nest.

Nestlings on hatching day.

Nestlings about 4 days old.

Nestlings about 6 days old.

Nestlings about 8 days old.

Nestlings about 10 days old.

Nestlings about 12 days old.

These descriptions, coupled with the accompanying photographs, should give you enough information to fully understand the growth and development of Purple Martin nestlings. Especially for those landlords who do not have the time or energy to do weekly nest checks during the breeding season, this information will allow you to estimate the age of your nestlings.

Hatching Day — The young break out of their shells by pipping along the equator of the egg with their bill. When the nestlings hatch, they are utterly featherless, blind, and completely helpless. They appear pink and still utilize their yolk sacs, the large round protrusions from their bellies that served as reservoirs of food while they were developing inside the egg.

Days 1–5 — At this age, the young are featherless and pink and have their eyes shut.

Days 6–9 — The young start to appear slate-gray along the wings, head, and back — the result of developing feather tracts beneath the surface of the skin. Small points start to appear along the trailing edge of the outer wings; these are sheathed feathers, called pin feathers. By the eighth day they may start to emerge on the tail as well. The eyes are still partially closed; they start to open about day 6 and open a little more each day.

Days 10–13 — On day 10 the eyes are open and the feathers start to burst out of their sheaths on the wings and tail, looking like black tips at the ends of the sheaths. These black tips get larger each day. Downy feathers on the body also begin to appear.

Days 14–16 — By day 14, emerging feather tips on wings and tail are about $1/4$–$1/2$ inch long and the body and head are covered with feathers. You can still see pin feathers on the back and the whitish sheaths of the wing and tail feathers. At this age the nestlings will begin to show fear when the nest compartment is opened.

Nestlings about 14 days old.

Nestlings about 17 days old.

Days 17–20 — No pin feathers or sheaths are visible. The pin feathers on the back have opened, revealing a purplish gloss that was not there before. You will notice a white powder on the feathers from the disintegrating feather sheaths. Throughout this period the tips of the wings gradually lengthen, but they do not yet reach the base of the tail feathers as seen from above.

Day 21–Fledging Day (28) — On day 21 the wing feathers extend to the base of the tail feathers. By day 26 they are about halfway down the length of the tail feathers, and by day 28 they extend to the tip of the tail or slightly farther. The weight of the nestlings peaks around day 20, so the young will actually start to lose weight slightly from now until they fledge at about 28 days. When the nestlings are this old, the nest compartment should not be opened, for the young might fly out prematurely.

Other Ways to Determine Nestling Age

If you have a colony that does not allow for easy access, there are important and easy-to-see behavioral clues that you can use to figure out what stage your birds are in.

Feeding – Depending on what kinds of insects the parents bring for their nestlings, an observer can determine roughly how old the birds are.

When the nestlings are still relatively young, the parents use a secretion in their mouth to form many small insects into a ball called a bolus. Although you cannot see the bolus directly, you will see a lot of movement in the parent's throat and mouth as it arrives at the nest hole. This movement may result from the parent forming the bolus or preparing to give it to a nestling. In studies, researchers have determined that young are fed these wads of food when they are between 1 and 15 days old.

If you see larger insects, like dragonflies or butterflies, pass from mouth to mouth, the nestlings are

Nestlings about 20 days old.

Nestlings about 22 days old.

Nestlings about 24 days old.

probably older. Dragonflies are the prominent item on the menu for young more than 15 days old.

Fecal Sac Removal — From the time they hatch to just a couple of days prior to fledging, the nestlings excrete white, membranous droppings called fecal sacs. These are most often removed from the nest by one or both of the parents and dropped a short distance away, usually within 50 feet of the colony. This is very easy to observe and is a sure sign of the continuing growth of the young.

Sometimes the fecal sacs are eaten by the adults, for they still contain food value and may help the adults get extra nutrition during this busy period when they have less time to feed for themselves.

Seeing the Nestlings — After the birds are large enough and strong enough, they will frequently come to the cavity opening to beg for food. These young will be about 18–20 days old. It will be increasingly easier to see them jostle for position and lean out as they get older.

A beautiful colony composed of gourds, near the end of the breeding season.

Additional Items for the Young

In addition to the insects that they eat, adult birds are busy bringing nestlings all kinds of other items to swallow, including crushed sea shells, glass, small stones, and gravel. This material provides the young with additional minerals and nutrients and is also stored in their gizzards to help with the digestion of hard-bodied insects. The gizzard is the muscular part of the stomach in which food is ground up by strong muscles, sometimes with the aid of foreign objects, called grit.

Leaving the Nest

Taking Flight

When young martins start to leave their nests be sure to take some time to sit back and observe. It is not only one of the more active periods at the colony, but there are some interesting and identifiable patterns of behavior to watch for as the young start to fledge. Easy-to-spot parent-young interactions are common and can be quite thrilling to observe.

As a landlord you should feel proud that the birds at your colony have reached this advanced stage and

As the young get older and approach fledging age, they spend a lot of time at the cavity entrance.

are on the verge of having had a successful breeding season.

Maiden Voyage

It generally takes 2–3 days for an entire brood to fledge, but occasionally this occurs in a single day. Typically the oldest bird or birds in a nest fledge first.

Fledging happens early in the morning, usually within the first couple of hours of sunlight and immediately after a parent has left the nest. The young take this cue and awkwardly flap out their very first glides of flight. Often only one bird leaves at a time, although two or three can leave together.

As they get closer to their departure date, the young birds become very excited. Premature fledgings are not uncommon in Purple Martin colonies and can be caused by a number of things, including jostling for food from an approaching parent, heavy parasite infestation, lack of food, oppressive heat, or a nest check by the landlord.

The fledglings follow their parents out of the nest but usually come immediately under attack from other martins. These mature martins may peck the young birds from above as they fly, or try to pull them from perches. These birds can also be seen pulling nestlings from nest holes and especially from the porches of houses just before the nestlings are ready to fledge.

Do not be alarmed; this is normal behavior, and the young are rarely injured in these encounters. The attackers are most often subadult males, some of whom have not bred that season, called floaters. Less often these birds are other parents. Floaters make life at the colony hard for fledglings, for they continually harass them, even after the juveniles have left the nest and found a perch nearby.

Most researchers think this harassment deters the young from returning to that particular breeding site.

A recently fledged Purple Martin. Note its overall stocky appearance and its strong resemblance to the adult female.

By eliminating the chance for a fledgling to imprint on a particular site, the adult birds have, in effect, ensured that these young birds will look elsewhere to breed in subsequent seasons, limiting nest-site competition in future years. While it has been proven that most young return to breed in close proximity to where they hatched, only about 15 percent or fewer actually return to the colony where they were born.

As you might observe, the parents of these harassed fledglings are very alert during this period and will vigorously defend their young from the attacks.

Family Gatherings

Fledglings may take off from the nest in different directions, landing in scattered locations, but the parents somehow manage to have them all together at the same perch by the afternoon of fledging days. Soft choo-calls are given by the young, perhaps aiding their discovery by parents. Young occasionally are misplaced or separated from their parents and siblings, but can be picked up by other parents.

The perch where a brood gathers is important and will be revisited by the same birds for the next few days. Finding these broods is not very difficult. Just walk or drive around the vicinity of your colony site and look for television antennas, utility wires, and exposed tree branches. In studies, the majority of these sites occur within 1 mile of the colony. The birds are very visible, for they are tightly clustered together. Despite their proximity to the colony, these sites are rarely visible from the martin housing, preventing floaters from bothering the fledglings.

The young assemble at this perch during the morning to preen, sunbathe, and be fed by their par-

"Floaters" are nonbreeding individuals at a colony. Because they are usually subadult males, like the one shown here, they are also called bachelors. These are the birds that harass fledglings when they first leave the nest.

ents. At first, the parents will perch right next to the fledglings and feed them large insects. The young quiver their wings slightly and give soft vocalizations when they see an approaching bird, and parents often give the food to the individual that starts quivering first.

Over the course of the next few days, the young are fed smaller insects, and in different fashions. First, the parents will hover before the perched young, dropping the food in the fledgling's mouth. Later, as the young become better fliers, they actually meet the parents in the air for in-flight transfers. By the fourth or fifth day after fledging, young are able to fly as skillfully as adults and start to catch their own food.

At dusk throughout this entire period, everybody returns to the colony to roost for the night. This will also happen in daylight during periods of bad weather, such as summer thunderstorms. Both parents are responsible for the young during this period, and both do an equal amount of work feeding the young and defending them from floaters and other birds who perch nearby.

The duration of this period differs slightly depending on how early or late the parents have bred. The earlier the birds fledge, as is the case in the southern locations, the more time they generally spend in this post-fledging phase before they are independent of their parents. Young that hatch later in the season, however, will spend less time in this phase, especially if other martins in the colony start to exhibit premigratory behavior. The difference is only a few days.

A parent feeding a fledgling at a gathering area. The young all quiver their wings as they beg for food.

Post-Breeding Defense

After the young have fledged, look for post-breeding defense of nest compartments. This is basically a replay of behavior exhibited at the beginning of the nesting cycle, but this time done mostly by floaters. Males acquire and defend territories against others and also advertise for mates. It has been suggested that this activity of acquiring and defending a territory imprints the location of the colony and even the exact location of prospective nest holes onto the participants. This may give them a slight edge next spring when they return.

According to researchers, this behavior is just as intense at the end of the breeding cycle as it is at the beginning, yet there are few fights, nesting material is not gathered, and the activity lasts only a few days.

What Happens After Breeding?

Communal Roosting

As the breeding season starts to wane, Purple Martins begin to gather in huge flocks, some of them numbering in the hundreds of thousands, to roost at night. These flocks also mark the beginning of the southward migration. Purple Martins do not migrate in large numbers. Rather, they leave as they arrive, in small, loose groups.

These flocks differ regionally. Some consist of local birds that are breeding, or have bred, in the area. Others, like the huge flocks in the South, especially

It is common to see lots of martins show up at your colony right before they all leave for South America. At this time, loose flocks will often visit neighboring colonies.

along the Gulf Coast, are made up of birds from all over the country, including birds that are in the process of moving north or south on their respective migrations (late-arriving subadults heading north will sometimes pass early-departing birds already moving south). Two larger known roosts, one in Louisiana, the other in South Carolina, are outlined below.

Martins frequently form preroosting flocks an hour or so before dusk on utility wires, antennas, or trees, often near open water. Here they feed, bathe, and preen. Right before dusk the birds leave this preroosting site and travel to another location, where they will spend the night. Sometimes these final locations include preroosting groups from different places and are consequently larger.

These groups also contain all of the young that successfully fledged that season, thus swelling the overall numbers. It is not uncommon to see large numbers of neighboring martins congregating at your colony during this period. This is why it can be good to play the dawnsong tape also at this time of year, for it may help attract young birds to your site the following year. The locations of these gathering sites may change over the course of a few weeks, especially toward the end of this period, as the birds ready themselves to migrate south.

Some martins roost in flocks throughout the breeding season; these flocks are small until the end of the breeding season, when they are joined by new birds.

The Big Roosts

There are premigratory and migratory roosts wherever there are Purple Martins; some are much larger than others. The ones in the South, for instance, tend to be larger than those in the North. This is because the southern roosts are usually made up of both local residents and birds that are in transit.

Even though martins often roost communally throughout the breeding season, this behavior is especially evident as they make their long journey south for the winter.

Two roosts merit special attention for their immense size; they are truly natural wonders and should not be missed. Seeing thousands of martins swirling in the air above you as they prepare to alight for the night is a breathtaking experience. These two exceptional roosts are the Lake Pontchartrain roost in Louisiana and the Lake Murray roost in South Carolina.

Lake Pontchartrain Causeway — This roost site actually comprises two roosts, one at the north end of the causeway and another at the south end. The causeway is 24 miles long and spans the width of Lake Pontchartrain in southern Louisiana, making it the longest over-water structure in the world.

The martins who congregate at the southern end are thought to be local breeders, while those at the north end are both local breeders and birds that are passing through. The roosts are largest from mid-June to mid-July, when there can be as many as 250,000 martins. The birds can be regularly seen here into September; by mid-October they usually have all left.

This is one of the more famous roosts and has both an observation deck from which you can look at the southern roost and special fencing along the rails of the causeway to keep martins from flying into oncoming traffic as they approach the roost.

Lunch Island, Lake Murray — This South Carolina roosting area has recently been made into a sanctuary through the combined efforts of three different groups, including the Columbia Audubon Society. The martins roost on Lunch Island, a 12-acre piece of land just off the shore in Lake Murray, west of Columbia. People estimate that 750,000 martins roost here at the peak of the season, in mid-July. Experiencing the full impact of this roost is possible only from a boat.

This is a roost in Mexico. It is thought that migrating martins, though they travel in small groups, roost at night in larger numbers.

Fall Migration

Purple Martins migrate to South America starting in summer. Southern martins begin this journey as early as June, while martins in the North may not begin migrating until August. In fact, it is possible that early southern-migrating martins in June pass subadult martins still migrating north. The birds do not leave in one large mass, as people often think, but in small, loose groups of several birds. By mid-October, most Purple Martins have left North America.

As is the case with their northern migration in the spring, there are many unanswered questions about the fall migration. Most research suggests that many Purple Martins spend their nonbreeding months in the state of São Paulo, in Brazil.

Wintering Activities

Located in southeastern Brazil, São Paulo has a terrain very similar to parts of North America, except that it has a tropical climate. São Paulo is densely populated, and its economy relies on industry and agriculture. Despite an abundance of rural landscape, most of the martins studied in this part of the country spend their nights in the middle of large cities. Most São Paulo urban areas have parks in the center of town with many trees. It is here that one can find large numbers of Purple Martins.

They create an enormous commotion at some of these locations and have prompted officials to take action against them in the past. Due to educational campaigns by South American officials, however, there is now a heightened appreciation of Purple Martins and the fascinating lives they lead. In fact, researchers claim that martins feed on a couple of very destructive crop pests while in South America.

There have also been studies at a roosting site in Manaus, a city deep within the Amazon Basin in northern Brazil. Here Purple Martins roost in the buildings of an oil refinery alongside Brown-chested and Gray-breasted Martins. Accounts given by researchers claim this is a very hostile environment. The sound level is incredibly high, the vibration of

Purple Martin winter range

This map shows where Purple Martins spend the winter.

Utility wires are one of the best places to spot large groups of martins in late summer just before they fly south.

pipes unnerving, and the whole place is lit with powerful floodlamps. Yet here is where they peacefully sleep, unbothered by the extremes around them.

Purple Martins inhabit a large portion of Brazil and other South American countries, including Colombia, Venezuela, and Guyana, and sections of Paraguay, Bolivia, Peru, Ecuador, French Guiana, and Suriname. There are only three countries in South America in which Purple Martins have never been seen: Argentina, Chile, and Uruguay. Obviously, there is much more to learn about the extent of their nonbreeding range.

Purple Martins spend most of their time in South America molting, feeding, preening, and bathing. The places they inhabit vary between sites similar to their breeding grounds in North America and sites deep within the tropical rain forest.

Martins will stay in South America until the return migration to their breeding areas in the spring. Purple Martins do not breed on their wintering grounds; they breed only in North America.

Molting

Molting is the process by which birds shed all of their old feathers and replace them with new ones. They need to do this because feathers, despite their hardiness, wear out over the course of a year. Going in and out of nesting cavities takes its toll on the feathers of Purple Martins, as does the normal accumulation of grit and the various parasites that feed on tiny feather particles.

Purple Martins undergo one complete molt each year. It begins after the breeding season, while the birds are still in North America, and is completed on the wintering grounds in South America. During migration, molting temporarily ceases, reserving the birds' energy for their arduous journey.

Purple Martins all molt in the same way. Feathers are not shed all at once, but in a very particular order. This ensures that the martins can still function normally while they are undergoing a molt. If you look for signs of missing feathers on the martins at your colony, you will most likely not find any. The molt is subtle, but sometimes you can spot where a wing or tail feather is missing.

Monitoring Your Colony

Be an Active Landlord

The more active you are as a landlord, the healthier your colony will be. Research clearly shows that landlords who actively monitor their housing have martins with higher fledging successes than landlords who do not monitor their colonies. Furthermore, active landlords will attract more martins and, if they keep up their good work, can easily increase the size of their colonies.

This section is designed to help you be an active, responsible landlord. There are many factors to consider, but once you learn what they are, caring for your colony gets much easier. Your objective should be to interact with your colony throughout the breeding season, so you can learn what is going on, prevent catastrophes, and enjoy success.

What Is Monitoring and Why Is It Important?

Monitoring your colony simply means periodically checking on the colony to make sure everything is going well; this includes performing nest checks. Looking inside the nests and recording what you see every 5 days or once a week will give you a lot of important information about your colony. You will be able to tell how many breeding pairs there are, how many eggs are laid, and how many young finally leave the nest. The only reliable way to gain this information, which tells you how healthy your colony is, is to conduct nest checks.

Furthermore, you will be able to see if there are any problems with nest-site competitors, martin predators, or parasites. This too is important information, for you will be able to take the right steps to avoid any problems that might lead the martins to abandon your colony.

You will also see firsthand all the things you have learned about the Purple Martin breeding cycle. Seeing the young quickly grow from tiny nestlings to full-feathered, full-bodied fledglings, for instance, is a great thrill.

Nest monitoring can only be done safely in housing that can be raised and lowered without tilting. The easier it is for you to look into each compartment the better, for this will save time and cause as little disruption as possible. If you do not have accessible housing, there are still ways to determine what phase of the breeding cycle different pairs are in (see the chapters on nest building and the nestling

Landlord Terry Suchma lowering a house for monitoring. One of the most important aspects of a good housing system is being able to raise and lower it without tilting it.

Inspecting every cavity is an important part of monitoring. Even though the birds may seem alarmed when you do this, things rapidly return to normal when you are finished.

phase), but you will not be able to accurately tell how many young are raised at your colony.

Purple Martins will never abandon their nests, young, eggs, or colony because of monitoring. The belief that once young or eggs have been handled by humans and have human scent on them they will be abandoned is not true; you can monitor your nesting compartments every day and the parents will not leave.

The reason for this is that most birds, including martins, have a very poor sense of smell. In addition, landlords are not perceived as predators by martins, they are merely minor "inconveniences" when doing nest checks. Purple Martins become increasingly bonded to a nest site as they go through the stages of building a nest, laying eggs, and raising young; therefore, only a major problem at the nest, such as something that threatened their own survival, would cause abandonment in the later stages of breeding.

Monitoring: Three Easy Steps

Step 1 — Monitoring your colony begins with becoming familiar with the housing — knowing how large the compartments are and how many are being offered to the martins. If you can label each compartment with a number or name, this is ideal. If you have a telescoping pole, mark the compass directions on the birdhouse so that when you put it back up after checking it, the compartments face the correct direction.

Step 2 — Walk under the housing whenever possible — once a day is ideal. Look for dropped items, like prey, feathers, eggs, or young. Also look at the housing itself to see if there has been any damage to it over the night. These daily walks under the colony will help familiarize you with the colony, and the martins will become accustomed to you.

Step 3 — Conduct nest checks. When you do nest checks, you basically want to look into every compartment and record what you see there, even if the compartments are empty. Use a clipboard with a record sheet on it, and record what you see in each compartment. (See page 96 for a sample nest record chart.) Keeping good records is the key to successful management. Having a history of records will help you see patterns over many years.

After nest checks, always make sure that the house is returned to the exact orientation it was in before you started. Otherwise, the birds will have trouble locating their own nests, and this may even cause nesting failure and abandonment of the site.

Being thorough is crucial to good monitoring. Make sure to record the contents of every compartment, even if some are empty.

Three Things to Observe During Nest Checks

Nest Material — You will find nests in different stages of completion, from a scattering of twigs to a nest complete with green leaves. Record the status of the nest each time you do a check.

Eggs — It is important to know how many eggs each breeding female lays and when they are laid. In particular, the day the first egg is laid, called the clutch initiation date, should be recorded. From this date, you can speculate when the nestlings will start to leave the nest — about 50 days later.

It is important to be very careful with the eggs; they are fragile and can be easily broken. If you have to poke around the nest to find them, or lift up nesting material, do it very carefully with the eraser end of a pencil or a small stick. If you find broken eggs, remove them. Make sure to include all eggs in your records, even if they are destroyed and will definitely not hatch.

Nestlings — Keeping track of the nestlings is important as well. From this you will be able to record their growth and health. Keep track of how many nestlings there are in each nest, including those that die over the course of the nestling period. Dead nestlings should be removed.

When Do I Monitor the Nests?

Start weekly nest checks when the martins have formed pairs and are beginning to build nests. The best time of day to monitor your colony is between late morning and early afternoon. During this time most of the adult martins forage for food away from the colony.

Nest monitoring should only be done during good weather. Nest checks during bad weather put stress on adult birds, eggs, and nestlings. If you know bad weather is coming, do nest checks a day or two early, or else wait out the cold spell.

Stop checking nests when the oldest nestlings in a house are about 20 days old, even though there are younger nestlings in other compartments of the same housing. Nest checks at this time may cause these older nestlings to fly out (fledge) prematurely, in which case there is a good chance they will not survive.

Nesting Success Rates

A recent study by the Purple Martin Conservation

Association showed that generally only 70 percent of eggs laid by martins actually hatch. Once hatched, only about 70 percent of the nestlings survived and left the nest.

These figures can vary due to weather conditions, availability of food, amount of monitoring done, and condition of the housing. But it is important to realize that the loss of eggs and nestlings is a natural part of martin life and that even in the best-managed colonies only about 50 percent of the eggs laid may result in fledged young and only 1–15 percent of these may return to the same colony the following year.

Troubleshooting

You will encounter many different situations while monitoring your colony. Here are the main problems encountered and what to do about them. Dealing with nest-site competitors, predators, and parasites are all discussed in the next three chapters.

Unhatched Eggs in the Nest — If an egg does not hatch, martin parents may remove it themselves. If they do not do this, and it is clear that the egg or eggs are not going to hatch, remove them from the nest.

Unhatched eggs result from a variety of causes; for example, they get cracked, they are unfertile, the embryo has genetic problems and fails to develop, or for some reason a female was unable to keep an egg warm enough on a particular day for it to be viable.

Dead Nestlings in the Nest — Likewise, the parents will usually remove smaller dead nestlings, or at least push them to the side of the nest. If this has not happened, you should remove the dead nestling.

Nestlings most frequently die because of lack of food, extreme weather, genetic problems, predation, or heavy parasite infestation

Older Nestlings in the Nest — If neighboring nestlings have wandered into other compartments, they should be replaced in their original nests. They can easily starve out neighbors, especially if the other nestlings are younger. Porch dividers prevent nestlings from wandering.

Nestlings Start to Jump Out During a Nest Check — This is common when the nestlings are getting ready to fledge from their nests. As a general

Make sure to return the housing to the correct height and orientation when you are done monitoring. Landlord Bill Dietrich is raising two of his houses here. The one on the left is on a telescoping pole, while the one on the right has a rope-and-pulley system.

rule, *nest checks should be discontinued in a house where the oldest nestlings are 20 days or older.*

When doing nest checks of nestlings nearing 20 days of age, carry along something to plug the entrance hole in case some try to leave the nest prematurely. Tie a long string around a rag, sock, Styrofoam cup, or something that will easily fit into a cavity opening. If any of the young show signs of being jumpy, gently stuff this plug into the hole as you finish the nest check, return the housing to its original position, and back off. Wait for several minutes so that the birds inside will calm down, then gently pull out the plug with the string. (You may even have to interrupt your nest check if the young seem especially active.) This is a good method of keeping the nestlings calm and avoiding premature fledging.

Finding a Nestling on the Ground — This is a common occurrence of martin life. There are many reasons why a nestling may end up on the ground. For instance, a weak nestling may be jostled out of the nest by its siblings in the rush for incoming food;

A homemade fallout shelter. Nestlings that have fallen out of their nests can be placed in these shelters and will be fed by any adult bird.

falls to the ground and you don't know which nest it belongs in, pick it up and place it in the shelter. The calling of the nestling will attract any parent bird, who will then feed it. Parents will not typically feed nestlings that are on the ground. The parents will continue to feed the nestling as it develops.

Helping Out

In addition to providing good housing and monitoring it, there are a few additional things some landlords do to help their martins.

Offering Crushed Eggshells — Offering crushed eggshells to martins provides the birds with grit and calcium. The grit helps grind up the bodies of hard insects in their digestive tract, and the birds need calcium for egg laying.

Offering eggshells is inexpensive and easy. Wash the eggshells, microwave them 3–5 minutes to kill any bacteria, and when they are cooled, grind them in a food processor until the pieces are the size of a pencil eraser. Place shallow mounds of eggshells in an open spot on an elevated tray feeder.

Offering Mealworms — While Purple Martins will not come to conventional bird feeders on their own, they can be induced to come to food placed on tray feeders. While this is certainly not a necessary measure to take as a landlord, it may help martins during a cold spell when insects are not available. Many people claim that feeding martins mealworms during prolonged cold spells tremendously increases their chances of survival. (Mealworms are sold at pet stores.)

You can offer mealworms to your martins the same way you offer eggshells — just place them in the open on an easy-access tray feeder. The martins may take several weeks to start using the feeder, but once they know about it they will come regularly. Some people put small trays of mealworms in each nest compartment, especially during the nestling phase. Experiment with different approaches and locations.

Many people think that offering food to the martins will make the birds dependent on humans and unable to hunt for themselves. This is untrue.

Cooling Off the Colony — There is little you can

parents may throw out a dying nestling; conditions inside the cavity may become so hot or parasite-infested that nestlings jump out for relief; and nestlings on the porch may get pulled to the ground by floaters.

The best thing to do if the nestling is still alive is to return it to the correct cavity. This can only be done if you have records that indicate how many nestlings are in each cavity. Putting a nestling back with young that are bigger or smaller can be disastrous. If the replaced bird is too young, it may fail to get any food and die; if it is too old, it may monopolize the food and starve out the other birds. If you are unsure where a bird came from, put the nestling in with other birds that are the same size.

You can also erect a fallout shelter with nesting materials inside. Some are commercially available, but you can easily construct one. It is just a protected cavity that an adult bird will come to and feed the nestling. Some people use an extra gourd with an extra-large opening, or two openings. If a nestling do to help the birds when it gets too hot. Having well-insulated, ventilated, white housing is beneficial in these conditions (this is the type of housing you should provide anyway). Some people have found that periodically spraying the housing with a fine mist from a garden hose helps, and the birds seem to like it. Parents will often wet themselves in nearby water or at a hose and then come back to the cavity to cool off the eggs or nestlings. If you spray the housing, be careful not to spray directly into the cavities — nestlings could drown easily, and soggy nest material takes a long time to dry. Wet nestlings can also suffer hypothermia if still unfeathered.

Cleaning Out at Season's End

As a general rule, you should clean out the housing at the end of the season, after the martins have left. Even though recent studies have shown that martins prefer cavities with old nests in them, these nests often have parasites that might over-winter and be a problem in the coming season. In addition, if you have wooden housing or natural gourds, the nests should be removed so as to prevent any rotting of the housing.

A basic cleaning by removing nest material, scraping, and a good hosing with water will result in a clean cavity. Some remnants of mud around the edges, a "nest scar," are good to leave, and may indicate to future martins that this cavity was successfully used before.

Spraying cleaned nest compartments and gourds with plain household ammonia and then closing off the openings for the winter may result in reduced numbers of nest parasites. The ammonia soon evaporates.

Wooden houses and gourds stored indoors for the winter may last longer. Aluminum houses can be left out for the winter with little harm to them, but should be lowered on the pole to reduce wind damage.

Rehabilitation

If you have a severely injured bird, the best thing to do is keep it in a dark, warm place — a closed shoebox with shavings in it is good — until you can get the bird to a licensed wildlife rehabilitator.

It is against state and federal laws to rehabilitate

This unusual-looking female martin is actually partially albino (leucistic). Although rare among martins, instances of completely albino birds have been documented.

wild birds without special wildlife permits. There are many wildlife rehab centers across the country; you can find one by calling your local nature center or state wildlife agency.

Dealing with Emergencies

If your martin housing falls over in a storm or is destroyed by hail, fire, lightning, vandals, or some other unfortunate circumstance, the best thing to do is repair or replace it as quickly as possible. Depending on what point of the breeding cycle the martins were in, they may start over, continue with their present efforts, or abandon the colony. The last usually happens only if they are too far along in the season to start over. Always make sure the housing is returned to the correct orientation.

Lightning rods can be bought and installed and will ground your colony. If you have questions about how to do this, talk to an electrician or go to an electronics store or hardware store — they should be able to help you.

Dealing with Competitors

Nest-Site Competition: A Real Threat

One of the most important things you can do as a landlord is keep your colony free of nest-site competitors. While the list of birds that will nest in Purple Martin housing is long, some species pose a more serious threat than others. Two species in particular that should not be allowed to use martin housing are House Sparrows and European Starlings.

These two competitors are nonnative birds, meaning that they are birds that were introduced to this country; they are not protected by law as are all of our native songbirds. Unfortunately, their success in many areas has directly caused declines in populations of native songbirds, especially secondary-cavity nesters like Purple Martins.

This section discusses how to deal with the problem of nest-site competitors, both native and nonnative.

House Sparrows

House Sparrows, members of the weaverbird family, were first introduced to North America by Nicholas Pike of the Brooklyn Institute in the spring of 1850. Although it is hard to believe, the original 8 pairs that were released in New York did not thrive. Another group of birds released 3 years later did very well and multiplied quickly. Over the next 20 years, House Sparrows were introduced in different parts of the country, and by 1940 their range was all of the continental United States and much of Canada.

House Sparrows pose a threat to martins because they not only usurp nesting cavities, they also destroy eggs, young, and sometimes adult martins. It is not uncommon to find a ruined nest in a colony that has House Sparrows. They will also start building their own nest on top of an active martin nest, destroying the eggs or young underneath.

What has been proven, both in scientific studies and in backyard colonies, is that House Sparrows will actively take over colonies. Studies show there are proportionately more Purple Martins at colonies where there are no House Sparrows. First-year colonies are especially vulnerable to House Sparrows, for these birds will keep inexperienced subadult martins from establishing themselves.

Furthermore, House Sparrows are resident breeders, meaning that they do not migrate, and will always be there first when martins return in spring.

The only way to effectively control House

Taking flight — what martins do best.

A female House Sparrow with nesting material. Although scenes like this suggest these two species can live side by side, studies reveal that Purple Martin breeding success declines at colonies where there are also House Sparrows.

Sparrows is to trap and permanently remove them. There are a number of box or wire traps commercially available that can be placed in and around the colony site to trap House Sparrows. When trapping birds, remember to continually check the trap. Be sure to release any protected native songbirds that might inadvertently be caught.

Alternatively, House Sparrows tend to avoid gourds, so if you want to have a colony of martins with no House Sparrows, but do not want to trap them, consider converting to a colony of gourds.

Another consideration is to be sure that you are not attracting House Sparrows at your bird feeders. You can do this by offering foods they will not eat, such as thistle, sunflower seed in the hulls, and suet, and by avoiding the use of mixed seed or any seed on the ground. This way, you can continue to attract most native songbirds and reduce your feeder's attractiveness to House Sparrows.

European Starlings

The European Starling was introduced to the United States in 1890. The first 60 pairs were released in Central Park in New York City that year, and then 40 more in 1891. The first nest was spotted, ironically, under the eaves at the American Museum of Natural History. Since then the starling has spread over the entire continental United States and north into Canada.

Like House Sparrows, European Starlings are aggressive nest-site competitors with Purple Martins. They are large, have strong bills, and will kill and eat Purple Martin nestlings and eggs. Similarly, they can build nests and successfully breed in a number of locations, and will quickly inhabit cavities in Purple Martin houses.

Because of their larger size, however, there is something landlords can do to discourage starlings.

They have much longer legs than martins and have trouble getting into smaller openings. There are starling-resistant, half-moon entrance holes that are designed to allow martins into the cavities but keep starlings out. See page 85 for more detail.

If you do not yet have these special entrance holes on your housing, control starlings by continually removing their nests and eggs or by other methods described for House Sparrows.

House Wrens

These birds are not as great a threat as House Sparrows and European Starlings, for they can usually be avoided by moving your Purple Martin or wren housing, or by not attracting House Wrens at all. Since House Wrens nest along wooded boundary areas, you can move your colony into a more open area to discourage them. If House Wrens enter your Purple Martin housing, close the compartment they are using and erect a bluebird-type nest box at the edge of the wooded area. Wait until they have taken up residence in the new house before reopening the compartment.

House Wrens are aggressive birds, and will puncture the eggs of nesting Purple Martins if they go unchecked. Remember, however, that these are native songbirds and should never be harmed. They play important roles in their resident ecosystems and have evolved there for hundreds of thousands of years.

House Finches

Although they are not widely recognized as nest-site competitors with Purple Martins, there is growing concern that House Finches, introduced to the eastern states from the western states in 1940, might become a threat to martins. There have been numerous accounts of House Finches living in both aluminum and wood housing and in natural gourds. It is unclear, however, what effect this competition will have on Purple Martin populations and their reproductive capabilities.

CHICKADEE / TITMOUSE   HOUSE SPARROW   BLUEBIRD   TREE SWALLOW   HOUSE WREN

Here are some nests of martin competitors to help you identify them. From left to right: chickadee or titmouse, House Sparrow, Eastern Bluebird, Tree Swallow, and House Wren.

A pair of Tree Swallows. Purple Martins and Tree Swallows can live side by side, but not in the same housing. Give Tree Swallows their own homes and they will be more successful.

House Finches do not actively attack martins or martin nests the way House Sparrows and starlings do, so there is not as great a concern over them. However, try to discourage House Finches from nesting in martin housing by closing up cavities in which they show an interest. House Finches are native songbirds and are protected by law.

Tree Swallows and Bluebirds

Tree Swallows, like martins, are members of the swallow family and are delightful to watch and have in one's yard. Sometimes, however, they will attempt to use Purple Martin housing. In fact, Tree Swallows will inhabit and defend an entire Purple Martin house, even when they only use one cavity.

Despite their much smaller size, Tree Swallows arrive earlier and are very aggressive toward Purple Martins, easily repelling them from prospective nesting sites if they have arrived first. To counter this, make sure to keep the housing closed until the martins have returned or are due to come through your area. As with the House Wrens, erect a bluebird box and wait until the swallows have taken up residence there. In this case, the house can be anywhere in the yard.

If you open your housing at the appropriate time for the martins but Tree Swallows are still its first inhabitants, simply close the housing again and wait until the swallows have started building elsewhere. Closing the housing for a time when subadult martins will be passing through your area will not eliminate your chances of starting a colony. Subadults travel through an area over the course of several weeks, so closing the housing for a few days in order to make it more attractive to potential martins is worth it.

In the West, there are Violet-green Swallows as well as Tree Swallows, and they can be dealt with in the same way.

Likewise, bluebirds can be easily coaxed into other housing in the same fashion. It is more uncommon for bluebirds to use martin housing.

Dealing with Predators

The Importance of Preventing Predation

It is natural for some Purple Martins to be lost to predators over the course of the breeding cycle, but losing too many can be serious. If a housing system is not properly outfitted with predator guards, it is not difficult for an owl, snake, or raccoon to do irreparable damage to a colony in a night or two.

It is important to protect martins from predators because the birds may abandon colonies that have been preyed upon.

This deep cavity made from PVC piping helps keep the birds out of reach of predators.

What to Do

Making sure your colony is as inaccessible as possible to all kinds of predators is the best way to protect the martins. Predators from the ground, such as raccoons and snakes, can be easily thwarted with a pole guard. Aerial predators, like owls and Fish Crows, can be stopped in two ways: by extra-deep cavities and by owl guards.

Pole Guards — Pole baffles that are available commercially come in a variety of models. Most are cone-shaped and fit on the colony pole. You can buy these from manufacturers and retailers, or you can make your own. Conelike baffles should be at least 36–40 inches wide and have a very shallow angle of pitch (about 5 degrees); they can be held in place by a clamp on the pole.

A 2-foot length of stovepipe suspended on the pole can be effective against some predators. It should be closed securely at the top with fine mesh screen, and the bottom of it should be at least 4 feet above the ground. A clamp placed on the pole and under the top of the stovepipe can hold it in place, or it can be attached to the bottom of the housing.

PVC pipe can also work as a pole guard. A 5-foot-long section of piping that is at least 4 inches in diameter is recommended. The base of the pipe should be flush with the ground and have a little sand spread around it.

By themselves, none of the pole guards totally prevent terrestrial predators from reaching the tops of poles. However, combining a baffle and PVC piping will make it extremely difficult for even the craftiest raccoons to ascend the pole.

Owl Guards — If the cavities in your housing are shallow, meaning they measure 6 inches or less from the entrance hole to the back wall, then owls can easily reach in and get the nestlings. In this case, you can put guards on the outside of the house that basically prevent the owls from being able to reach the nest. These guards usually consist of vertical bars placed across the porches of the housing and spaced far enough apart to let the martins pass through easily (3 inches apart). By using these guards, you are in effect deepening the cavities so that owls cannot reach the martins inside. Owl guards are commercially available for a number of houses or can also be constructed at home using wooden dowels.

Other ways to owlproof your housing include making nest compartments deeper, and securing nest-access doors with pieces of coat-hanger wire placed under each door spring (to keep owls from ripping the doors off).

Deep Cavities — Basically, the deeper the cavities, the safer the martins and their young ("depth," in this context, refers to the distance from entrance hole to back wall). Many researchers believe that if given the chance, nesting martins will use the least accessible spot in a cavity to build their nest and raise their young, out of the reach of predators.

In the past, it was believed that by deepening cavities you were inviting starlings in to build nests. One reason conventional housing has shallow compartments is that research shows that starlings are less likely to nest in small compartments because of their own nesting requirements. With the invention of the starling-resistant entrance, however, deeper cavities can be constructed and used without your having to worry about starlings.

What Does Not Work

There are a variety of strategies that people use to repel predators that do not work. Lubricating the pole with axle grease, petroleum jelly, or Teflon spray does not work in repelling snakes, raccoons, or other climbing predators. The only predators that are foiled by petroleum jelly are fire ants.

The Most Common Purple Martin Predators

A number of different animals will prey on Purple Martins. While it may be impossible to eliminate all predation at your colony, the preventive steps you take will help reduce it considerably.

Predator guards like the two pictured here are the most effective way to prevent ground predators such as raccoons and snakes from reaching your housing. The one above is commercially available; the one below is homemade.

Raccoons — These animals are ubiquitous throughout the range of the Purple Martin and will not hesitate to prey on easily available martins. Raccoons are intelligent and surprisingly agile animals and cannot be overestimated. Preventing them from being able to climb the house pole is the best way to discourage them. An effective pole guard or two will do the trick. Signs of raccoon predation include widely spaced scratch marks on wooden poles or on wooden houses, and heads and/or wings of martins on the ground in the area.

Owls — The most common owls that prey on Purple Martins include Great Horned Owls, Eastern Screech Owls, Barred Owls, and Barn Owls. Along with raccoons, these aerial predators are the biggest threat to martin colonies, rangewide.

Keeping the nest out of reach is the best strategy against these birds. They have surprising strength, and the larger ones can easily rip the doors off conventional aluminum housing unless they are tightly secured. Owl guards and deep cavities are the best defense against these birds.

In the aftermath of an attack, look for both martin and owl feathers (the latter's are usually brown and more downy than the martin feathers) around and below the compartments. The nest will typically be very messy and scattered as well. If there is an exposed perch nearby, the owl might have used it to eat its prey. There may be owl pellets — wads of undigestible material like feathers and bones — on the ground beneath such perches.

Snakes — A number of snakes are threats to martins, including the black rat snake, yellow rat snake, fox snake, and corn snake, which are all different species in the genus *Elaphe*. Contrary to what most people believe, these predators are excellent climbers and can easily negotiate poles. They also have the ability to stretch their bodies out to climb overhangs.

The best way to discourage snakes is with a stovepipe baffle described earlier in this chapter. A cone-shaped pole guard may also be effective as long as it is at least 36–40 inches in diameter. Snakes are more of a problem in the South than at northern colonies.

Unlike most other predators, snakes leave very few clues that they have visited a colony, except, of course, for the missing birds. Frequent nest checks will disclose some snakes. Certain snakes will enter

The raccoon is perhaps the most common terrestrial martin predator. Raccoons' abilities can never be overestimated, so outfit any pole with a predator guard.

Owl guards fit on the outside of conventional houses and prevent owls and other avian predators, like Fish Crows, from being able to reach the nests. The one on the left is available commercially, while the one on the right is made out of simple wooden dowels.

a compartment and eat the birds, then stay there until they are hungry again, then raid one or more other compartments. If you come across a snake in a compartment, gently coax it out with a long stick. Do not harm the snake.

Hawks and Falcons — Hawks and falcons that may prey on martins throughout the country include the Sharp-shinned Hawk, Cooper's Hawk, Northern Goshawk, American Kestrel, Merlin, and Peregrine Falcon.

However, it is rare for these hunters to spend their time trying to capture agile martins when there are other, slower birds around. If it does happen, though, it usually occurs in the immediate vicinity of the colony, when martins are flying slowly. In fact, it is thought that one of the reasons martins prefer their housing out in the open is so they can make faster approaches to the colony, thus making themselves harder to catch. Hawks attack mostly in the air — but occasionally they catch a martin that is perched on a house or clinging to the entrance of a gourd.

Crows and Gulls — American Crows and especially Fish Crows are becoming greater threats to martin colonies. Unlike owls, which hunt at night, crows will visit colonies during the day; but like owls, crows can be thwarted by owl guards and deeper compartments. Fish Crows are probably the biggest threat to martins in southern states, especially Florida.

Some species of gulls have been known to kill martins as well. They can be prevented the same ways that other aerial predators are — owl guards and/or deep compartments. Neither crows nor gulls can effectively raid houses without porches or raid gourds, for they are too heavy to hold on to the entrance hole and reach in at the same time.

Roadrunners — In the South, especially in Texas, Roadrunners have been known to prey on Purple

Martins. They can likewise be held at bay with owl guards and/or deep cavities.

"Nest Robbers" — Blue Jays, grackles, starlings, House Wrens, and House Sparrows are among the birds that will steal eggs and young from Purple Martin nests. Sometimes they merely puncture eggs. Only two of these — starlings and House Sparrows — are not protected by law. The others are all protected and should never be harmed or killed.

Except for the all-important task of keeping starlings and House Sparrows away from your colony, there is little you can do to protect your colony from these birds. Martins at a colony will typically chase off larger birds that might pose any kind of threat, including jays and grackles. Also, gourds and houses without porches are harder for grackles and jays to enter.

House Cats — House cats can be incredibly crafty.

Fortunately, they cannot climb metal poles very well. They are not a major threat to Purple Martins because the martins spend so little of their time on the ground.

However, if the martins are collecting nesting material, a cat can easily catch them. Make sure that when the martins are on the ground collecting nesting material, they are out in the open. Any nearby shrubbery or other cover can provide a cat with the position to make an easy kill. If you provide eggshells for the martins, be sure they are offered on an elevated tray.

Squirrels and Opossums — These mammals are not serious threats to martins, but they should be kept away from colonies by the same means you keep raccoons away — a pole guard.

Squirrels are incredible climbers and leapers. They can easily get onto a housing system from nearby trees, branches, structures, and wires. Some species

These Purple Martins are in gourds, which helps them avoid predation by crows.

An adult male near the colony site. If a colony has been attacked by predators, martins will usually leave. Sometimes they stay nearby but do not enter the nesting cavities.

will use the martin house for their own nests. It is very rare for a squirrel to kill martins, but they can definitely usurp nesting cavities. They will be prevented from climbing a pole by pole guards. In some areas, flying squirrels can be a problem, but if you have pole guards and your colony is placed far from tall trees, they will not be able to reach the nests.

What to Do If Your Colony Has Been Attacked

You should be able to tell if your colony has been attacked from the behavior of the martins. If they seem particularly vocal and alarmed and refuse to land on the housing or enter cavities, this most likely indicates a predation. There is a chance that the predator is still around, especially if it is a snake. Martins will not land on housing if they know that a snake is there.

Short of moving your site, there is really only one thing you can do if your colony has been attacked by a predator — keep it from happening again. But do not wait until a predator attack has taken place to install guards — they should go on when the housing is first erected, even if you think you will not have any problems.

If the entire colony has been wiped out, chances are that martins will not return for several years. If this happens, you might try moving your housing to a different, suitable location nearby. Other martins may consider this a "new" site and establish a colony.

Controlling Parasites

What Can You Do?

You may wonder, as a Purple Martin landlord, if there is anything that you can do to help your birds during the nestling phase. The answer is yes. Minimizing parasites is a help, because nests that have too many parasites produce fewer young. If needed, you can do one or two nest replacements during the nestling phase. Or you can sprinkle plain, unadulterated diatomaceous earth in the nest (con-

tains no pesticides). Both of these strategies are safe, nontoxic ways to minimize the number of parasites.

The most common parasite in martin nests is the blowfly. Adult blowflies lay their eggs in the nest of a Purple Martin. The eggs hatch and the blowfly larvae feed on small amounts of the blood of the nestlings, especially at night. They are easily controlled by nest replacement and removal of any larvae from the nestlings.

Nest Replacement — When and How to Do It

Nest replacement is simply the removal of the original nest in a nesting compartment or gourd and its replacement with a bed of new, clean, dry material. Doing 1–2 nest replacements over the course of the nestling phase is the safest and most effective way to minimize blowflies.

There are several materials that can be used for the replacement nest, including long pine needles, dried lawn clippings, soft wood shavings (not cedar), wheat straw, and pine shavings. The shavings can be purchased at pet stores, and the wheat straw is available in feed stores and lawn-and-garden centers. If you have a lawn that is frequently mowed, save the clippings and then dry them out; this is cheap and resourceful. Avoid materials such as sawdust, which takes a long time to dry if it gets wet. Be generous when adding nesting material, for you want it to be thick enough that the young will not scrape it away.

Nests should be replaced once when the nestlings are between 8 and 12 days old, and then again when they are 18–20 days old. The second replacement will help eliminate parasites that have arrived since the first replacement. It is unwise to do nest replacements before the nestlings are 8 days old, because it is thought that the original nest provides the younger nestlings with certain thermoregulatory needs for

A martin at a gourd. Parasites are a natural but often unseen part of the lives of Purple Martins. As a landlord, you can take steps to help keep the numbers of parasites to a minimum.

Most of the parasites that live on nestlings or in nests are undetectable, as in this picture, to the casual observer. Blowfly larvae, when mature, are large (about $^3/_8$ inch long) and dull red, and can be found in the nest or attached to the nestlings.

growth. It should also not be done after the young are 20 days old, because the older birds are likely to jump from the nest prematurely if they are disturbed too much after this age.

Nest replacements are easiest in compartments with slide-out trays. It is obviously impossible to do nest replacements in houses that do not have easy compartment access (such as individual doors for every bird entrance hole) or in gourds that do not have side or rear access doors.

When changing nests, carefully remove the nestlings from the original nest and place them in a dark, warm place — a closed shoebox with some tissue or dry lawn clippings or other replacement material is good. It is important, especially with the older birds, to keep them as calm as possible. If they seem very excited and you fear that they will try to leave the nest prematurely when they are returned to their housing, refer to page 63 for tips on helping prevent this.

The original nesting material can go in the trash or a compost pile, but keep it away from the colony. Sometimes parasites can find their way back to a compartment if they are expelled too close to the colony.

Form a shallow bowl with the new material, pro-

viding a space that closely resembles the discarded nest. Put the slide-out tray back in the house, or gently place the new nest in the gourd, and then carefully lay the nestlings back in the nest. Once again, remember that none of these activities will harm the nestlings or cause the adults to abandon the nest.

This is the best and safest way to help limit the numbers of blowflies and possibly nest mites that infest the nestlings at your colony. It is nontoxic and will therefore do no long-term damage to the birds as would chemical strategies of controlling the parasites. It is widely believed that you should not use Sevin or sulfur as a control measure and that it is safer to replace the original nests with new material instead.

Occasionally the parents will reject the new nest material and push it aside, exposing the metal floor on aluminum houses. This slippery surface can cause the nestlings' legs to splay outward, and this is not good for them. To avoid this, you can cut a piece of plastic mesh, available in craft and needlework stores, to fit the floor of the compartment. This material has small holes that the nestlings can grip with their claws and prevent leg splay.

Landlords who choose a more passive role in

managing their colonies can take two steps that help the birds at the beginning of the season: before the martins arrive, clean the house well; and put clean, dry bedding, such as pine needles, dry lawn clippings, or pine shavings, in each compartment to aid and further attract the birds.

Because Purple Martins and the insects and mites that parasitize them have coevolved, many landlords feel there is no reason for controlling parasite populations. The fact that most Purple Martins use human-supplied housing, however, may artificially increase the chances that nestlings are parasitized. Especially in cases of wet, cold weather or hot, dry weather, when nestlings may be weakened, the abundance of hosts might work to the advantage of certain parasites, making it easier for them to transfer from one host to another or from one nest to another. Whatever decision you make, it is important to know about parasites and how they affect Purple Martins.

If you choose to take a more passive role, perhaps an apt strategy would be to do nest changes only under the worst circumstances, such as when there is a particularly cold or wet season, or if there seems to be a high population of blowflies in your area.

Diatomaceous Earth

Freshwater or agricultural diatomaceous earth is another safe way to help minimize parasites, especially blowflies. If there are many blowflies at your colony, simply sprinkle a teaspoon of diatomaceous earth around the outer edges of each nest. Do this once when the nestlings are about 8–10 days old and then again when they are about 18–20 days old. Do not put diatomaceous earth directly onto the nestlings, for this may irritate or injure them, and do not spray it in, for the birds might inhale it. When you buy it, be sure to get freshwater or agricultural diatomaceous earth and not the saltwater diatomaceous earth put in swimming pools or the kind sold at hardware stores that also contains pesticides.

Diatomaceous earth is simply the skeletal remains of tiny marine animals, called diatoms, that have been ground into fine dust. While harmless to humans and other large animals, the sharp particles of the dust cut into the outer shell of the insects, causing them to die. In any case, avoid inhaling it or getting it in your eyes.

Nest replacements are the best and safest way to minimize the number of parasites in a nest. Gently cupping your hand over the nestlings as you do a replacement will help keep them calm, especially as they get older.

An adult female martin. Martins have parasites that live on their feathers throughout their lives. The natural behaviors of preening and molting help keep parasites to a minimum.

Blowfly Life Cycle

Blowflies are insects and perhaps the most common and destructive of the Purple Martin parasites. It is not the adult flies that parasitize the martins but the larvae. Adult female blowflies lay eggs in the nests of Purple Martins and other secondary-cavity nesting species, including bluebirds and Tree Swallows. After these hatch, small larvae (usually about 1/4–1/2 inch long) that are a translucent, pearly white color attach themselves to the nestlings and suck some blood from them. This usually happens at night, when the larvae can go undetected by the parent martins, especially if there is only moderate infestation in the nest. This is why blowfly larvae are difficult to see and why some landlords might assume there is not a problem in their colony.

During periods of heavy infestation, however, as during warm, wet weather, the larvae will feed at all times of day and will be very easy to spot. After they feed on the nestlings, the larvae appear dull red. If you can see blowfly larvae on the nestlings' wings, belly, or legs or in the nest, remove and destroy them.

After about 2 weeks of intermittently feeding on the nestlings, the larvae will pupate and turn into brownish-purple pupal cases. After 10–11 days in this form, the cases will open and hatch adult flies. By this stage the flies are harmless to the nestlings and will leave as soon as they can.

Other Parasites

There are actually dozens of insects and arachnids that parasitize Purple Martins, both adults and nestlings. Some of them live on the birds, among the feathers, while others live only in the nest. Nest replacements will help minimize the destructive capabilities of most of these parasites, as well as minimizing blowfly populations.

Adverse Weather and Martins

What Is Bad Weather for Martins?

Purple Martins are weather-sensitive birds, and adverse weather is the cause of death of thousands of martins every year. Adverse weather for martins is any prolonged period of cool weather either with or without rain and any prolonged period of hot, dry weather. This weather reduces the presence of flying insects, the staple of the martin diet, and therefore weakens the birds and can even cause death. Adverse weather usually occurs in spring, just as the birds are first arriving on their breeding grounds, but it can also occur in summer.

Most people think that cold weather is what kills martins, but in fact they can easily withstand cold as long as they can get food. It is not the cold weather per se, but the lack of food and the need for more energy to keep warm in cold weather, that is the real problem for the birds.

There are two things that landlords can do to help their martins during adverse weather. One is to supplement their food in either hot or cold spells and the other is to help them stay warm during cold spells.

Feeding Martins Mealworms

As a landlord, you can feed your martins mealworms anytime there is a long cold or hot spell that inhibits the activity of flying insects. While cold spells usually occur when martins first arrive, in the North they can also happen later in breeding, even during the nestling phase.

To some people, putting out mealworms may seem like a lot of trouble, but think of all the effort many of us make to feed birds seed in winter. We spend hundreds of dollars and considerable time, so why not spend a little more time and effort to help out the martins in summer? Many Purple Martin landlords are beginning to see that feeding martins is an essential part of their stewardship. It may be a bit more labor, but it is a labor of love that is helping save Purple Martin lives. (See page 64 for more information about offering mealworms to martins.)

Supplying Heat Inside the Housing

In times of cold weather, Purple Martins, like many other birds, exhibit a behavior known as communal roosting. Large numbers of martins will roost and rest within the same compartment in the house, all sharing their body heat and thereby conserving energy and saving the lives of individuals during these demanding times. By communally roosting in warmed housing, martins may be able to extend their lives by a day or two when unseasonably cold weather continues.

Purple Martin landlords can supply heat to their housing by placing one or two 60–70-watt lightbulbs in the empty compartments of a house. It is preferable to use a central compartment so that the heat will warm as many other compartments as possible. Use duct tape to close up the entrance hole where the bulb is, to keep the warmth in and the birds out of this compartment. Turn on the lights during the days and nights of cold weather.

The number of lightbulbs needed depends on the size of the martin housing. Larger houses, with 20 or more compartments, may need two bulbs, while smaller houses may need just one. You can even place the lights on timers so that they come on only at night if it is only the nights that are especially cold. Be sure to use safety outdoor extension cords and be particularly careful in wet conditions.

Incredible as it might seem, the heat from one small lightbulb will radiate to the floors, ceilings, and walls of the house and help keep the resident mar-

Cool, rainy weather is tough on martins.

tins warmer and hopefully alive long enough to survive. A view of these birds inside the house would show all the birds huddled close to the source of warmth.

In northern latitudes, placing lightbulbs in martin housing can be a regular springtime ritual. They can easily be removed when the weather moderates.

This chapter was written by Terry Anne Suchma. For more on her work, see Resources.

Innovations to Your Colony

Change: A Constant Feature

If there is one constant among martins enthusiasts, it is that they are always changing their colonies. This is one of the joys of being a landlord and man-

As soon as landlords become comfortable with managing the colony they have, they often expand. Here are two proud landlords who have added housing over the years.

aging a colony. Changes may include moving the housing to a new location, adding new housing, replacing old housing with something completely different, or making improvements and modifications on what you already have. This chapter will tell you the basics about making these kinds of changes to your colony.

Martins are sensitive to changes and may leave a colony if changes are made too abruptly. As a general rule, it is best to make any changes, moves, or additions gradually, even over the course of a couple of years. The only change acceptable to martins during the breeding season is the addition of new housing. Colonies should not be moved, replaced, or modified during the season, unless absolutely necessary.

Moving Your Colony

There may come a time when you have to move your colony. Maybe a favorite tree has grown too close and you do not want to trim it, or an addition is being made to your house, or a new house is going up right where the colony is.

If you have never had martins nesting at your site, this is not a problem — just move it. If you have an active site with breeding martins, moving the colony can be very disruptive and should be done with great care.

To make a move, put up the new housing at least one year before the old housing is coming down. This way, the martins will know it is there and might even start using it. The next season, do not put up the old housing, so the martins will move to the new site.

Sometimes people do not have a year or two to make a move like this, or do not have new housing to offer but need to find a new location for the current housing. If this is the case, just move the housing and hope for the best. It is best if the move can be anticipated and done before the martins have

This is a good way to expand your colony — add another house 10-15 feet away from the original colony.

arrived. If you can, move the colony slowly over the course of a few seasons, instead of all at once.

Replacing Your Purple Martin Housing

At some point you will probably want to replace existing housing with something new. This usually happens when you want to improve the housing you offer or when housing starts to wear out.

Housing replacement should be done in the off-season, after the birds have left for the year. If the new housing you are offering is the same design as the old, simply replace the old with the new. The new housing should be in place when the martins return, and occupy exactly the same space the old one did. The closer you can match the two, in height and especially in compass orientation, the better. Returning martins have a real knack for remembering exactly where they nested the year before, even when the housing is not up yet!

If the new housing is of a different design, follow the same guidelines as for moving a colony — try to offer both systems for at least one season, so the birds can get used to the new housing. Since it does not matter how close colonies are to each other, you can put the new housing within a few feet of the old.

Expanding Your Colony

If you have a colony that you are able to manage well and you simply want to add housing to what you have, go ahead and do it. New housing should be put close to existing housing, at least as close as 10–15 feet. It does not matter how close, as long as there is direct flight access to all nest holes. An easy and inexpensive way to do this is to add gourds. They can be hung from the bottom of traditional houses or hung on wires between poles.

It is important, though, that the housing previously used by the martins not be disturbed unless you are replacing it.

When to Expand — Colonies should be expanded when you are able to manage your current colony well and feel that you can handle the extra compart-

ments. In many ways, it is always good to have more than one house up. This provides protection for the perpetuation of the colony in case one house is damaged by a storm or preyed upon.

If you have traditional housing, try adding porch dividers; this can increase your occupancy rate by discouraging individual males from defending more than one nest hole. Normal housing without porch dividers usually has about a 50 percent occupancy rate due to male territoriality. With porch dividers between adjacent nest holes, occupancy rates can reach 75–100 percent. Porch dividers have the added advantage of keeping nestlings from wandering into other compartments.

The healthiest colonies are those that can be managed well. As a landlord, aim for this goal instead of having as many pairs as possible or having the biggest housing available.

Other Ways to Expand — There are other ways to expand as a landlord. You can help put up colonies

This is a good example of improving your housing. The PVC pipe houses added to this colony are especially deep and thus offer the birds more protection from predators reaching in.

A house with homemade owl guards and an extra perch on top. Perches on top of housing are easy and inexpensive to add and are well used by the martins.

in other places, for example. If you have a second residence, or work somewhere that would be great for a colony, why not try establishing a colony in one of these places?

Whenever possible, try to educate people about Purple Martins and other birds. Encourage friends and neighbors to put up Purple Martin housing. Showing them your colony and sharing your experiences with them is an excellent way to do this.

Improving Your Housing

There are always improvements to be made to Purple Martin housing. Conventional houses and gourds alike can be inexpensively modified to offer healthier compartments for the martins. Starling-resistant entrance holes can be put on houses and gourds. The compartments inside conventional houses can be enlarged as well.

With gourds, rain canopies can be installed above the holes to prevent water from coming in, and access doors can be added to the side or rear, making the compartments much more accessible for monitoring and for cleaning at the end of the season.

Starling-Resistant Entrance Holes — Believe it or not, there is such a thing as a starling-resistant entrance hole. This is a half-moon-shaped hole 3 inches wide and $1^3/_{16}$ inches high, slightly smaller than what martins generally prefer. An innovative landlord named Charles McEwen, of Moncton, New Brunswick, Canada, came up with the design and did the first test runs. Since then, thousands of landlords have tried his invention and claim that it works.

Research suggests that these smaller entrance holes take some adjustment on the part of the martins but seem to be quickly accepted.

If you are unsure, however, you can make the

Housing should always be maintained – joints become loose, nuts and bolts rust, wires start to wear thin, and wooden walls lose their paint and start to rot. In this picture, the hangers for gourds are being replaced.

entrance holes, for they may deter birds that first explore your site. On established sites, the birds are more attached to the colony and will tolerate the altered entrances.

Enlarged Compartments — Recent research shows that enlarged compartments are preferred by martins. Given the opportunity, martins will nest in the least accessible part of a cavity, making them safer from the reach of predators.

If you have a conventional house with cavities measuring 6 x 6 x 6 inches, it is not too difficult to modify the house so that compartments are doubled in size, even if it is aluminum. Although this change will reduce the number of available cavities in the house, it will offer the martins a safer environment.

Start by looking at the floor plan of the house and figuring out how to double the size of each compartment. Walls can sometimes be removed or new holes cut through interior walls between adjoining cavities. These connecting holes should be at least $2\frac{1}{4}$ inches in diameter. When the two cavities are joined, plug up one of the entrance holes and you have an extra-large compartment. The first room becomes an entryway and the second is where the nest is built.

These design strategies will obviously differ from house to house, but they can be accomplished with any design, including hexagonal houses. Of course, you can also create larger compartments by building your own martin house.

Textured Subfloors — Most subfloors and floor surfaces, especially in the commercially made houses, are hard and smooth. This is a problem for nestlings whose nest becomes scattered. When they have nothing to grip onto with their feet, their legs can develop poorly and splay outward.

To counter this, some landlords add textured surfaces to the floor, to give the nestlings something to grip. The best material is plastic mesh, available at craft and needlepoint stores. Carefully glue this material to the bottoms of the cavities at the corners.

Improvement to Gourds — To be able to get into your natural gourds to do easier nest checks and nest replacements, you can install an access door on the side of each gourd. This is a fairly simple addition and can be done inexpensively.

Andrew Troyer, experienced landlord and builder

new hole opening adjustable, so that you can gradually reduce the opening to the minimum $1\frac{3}{16}$-inch height after the martins have started to build the nest. This works because once the martins have started building nests they become more invested in holding on to a certain cavity and will be more tolerant of getting used to new openings. Adjustable starling-resistant holes can also be installed on gourds, but they must be individually made to fit.

If you are trying to attract martins for the first time, you may not want to use starling-resistant

A beautiful hexagonal wooden house. Designs like this can be modified to include larger compartments and starling-resistant entrance holes; stationary poles can also be replaced by pulley-and-winch poles.

of the T-14 martin house, has come up with the idea of using the screw-tops of plastic jars as an access hole. Jars for this purpose can be found wherever plastic food containers are sold.

To do this, first cut the jar collar from the jar; then, using 2 screws, screw the jar collar to the gourd and caulk all around the seam; finally, place the lid back on the jar. The screw-off top can then be your access to the gourd.

It is good to use a wide-mouth plastic jar top, about 4 inches in diameter, so that you can easily monitor the nest. In the end, paint the outside of the plastic jar white to match the rest of the gourd.

These are just some of the more common and popular changes landlords have been designing and making. Coming up with new designs and innovative ideas is part of the fun and challenge of being a landlord.

Western Purple Martins

Western Versus Eastern — A Big Difference

This book is designed for anyone who wants to attract Purple Martins. However, you should be aware that there are major differences in behavior of Purple Martins in the East versus those in the West. The familiar vision of Purple Martins living in large colonies in multicompartment housing is only true for birds east of the Rocky Mountains. Purple Martins in the West and Southwest are not only less common, but also live singly in natural cavities,

This female Purple Martin is about to enter a potential nest site in a saguaro cactus. Purple Martins typically nest in holes about 20 feet from the ground.

single houses, and gourds. These birds can be monitored in the same fashion as eastern martins.

Therefore, the Attracting Martins portion of this book is for people who live east of the Rocky Mountains. The other sections on behavior and life history apply to all Purple Martins.

Even though this book is filled with pictures of colonies from eastern sites, do not be discouraged if you live in the West. It is still possible to attract martins to single houses and, in the West, they nest in a wide array of habitats, from the desert to lush riverside valleys. Several single-unit houses can be placed at varying heights on different sides of a tall pole.

Variations on a Theme

There are three main subspecies of Purple Martins. (A subspecies is a population that differs slightly from others.) The martins that we are most familiar with and that come to artificial housing in the eastern part of the continent are members of the subspecies *Progne subis subis*. This is by far the most abundant and widespread subspecies and lives east of the Rocky Mountains.

In addition, two less abundant subspecies live in the West. They are called *Progne subis arboricola* and *Progne subis hesparia*.

Western Subspecies

Progne subis arboricola — Frequently referred to as the "montane" subspecies of martins, these birds breed at high elevations, often in mountain ranges. Members of this group are actually a bit larger than eastern martins, but this difference is slight and will not be apparent to the casual observer.

Birds of this subspecies have been spotted along the coast in southern Alaska, British Columbia, Washington, and Oregon. They have also been seen

A pair of martins atop a cactus. The males of this southwestern subspecies, *Progne subis hesparia,* appear similar to eastern martins, while the females tend to be a bit lighter in their plumage.

farther inland in Washington, Oregon, British Columbia, Idaho, and Utah. They are not common, and it may be that logging, cosmetic removal of snags on trees, and competition from starlings are the reasons for their sparse populations.

There are campaigns to interest more people in martins in states like Washington and Oregon, especially close to the coast. The Columbia River Valley and Willamette Valley both provide an abundance of excellent habitats for martins, as do the other lush valleys of the Pacific Northwest.

These martins can be attracted to artificial housing, so if you are a martins enthusiast living in the Northwest, your case is not completely lost. It might be difficult to attract them, but it can happen.

If you know that there are martins nesting in human-made housing near you, the best strategy would be to emulate that kind of housing. This may help, because most western martins, unlike their eastern counterparts, are not "used to" artificial housing and are less likely to bend to the whims of individual landlords. For instance, if there are mar-

tins nearby nesting in single-unit houses, offer similar housing on your property.

Progne subis hesparia — This subspecies is believed to live primarily in the Sonoran Desert and other arid places, such as Baja California. It is the smallest of the subspecies. Unfortunately, for aspiring landlords at least, these martins hardly ever come to artificial housing. If you live in the desert and are trying to attract martins, your chances are slim. Some researchers attribute this to the poor insulative capabilities of artificial housing relative to the cool insides of natural cavities. Temperatures in this region are extremely high during the breeding season, and nestlings would consequently suffer in aluminum or wood housing.

However, these martins do nest in holes excavated by woodpeckers in saguaro cactuses. Populations of this subspecies may be declining due to there being fewer saguaro cactuses. Therefore, if you have these wonderful cactuses on or near your property, make every effort to save them.

The History of Purple Martin Colonies

Where It All Started

At one time, thousands of years ago, eastern Purple Martins nested in natural cavities — excavated woodpecker holes, crevices in scraggly rock faces, or natural cavities in old trees — much the way

An adult female at a gourd. Unpainted gourds may be what were first used to attract martins. To ensure a cooler compartment, it is now widely recommended that you paint gourds white.

they do presently in the West. Now, however, Purple Martins east of the Rockies nest almost exclusively in colonies in human-made housing. How and why did these changes occur?

Why Did the Birds Change Their Behavior?

The answer to this question is somewhat unclear but begins with the fact that Purple Martins have been managed by humans longer than any other species of bird in North America. It is believed that some of the southeastern Native American tribes, including the Chickasaw and Choctaw, started putting up hollowed-out gourds for these birds hundreds and maybe thousands of years ago.

Since then, all kinds of people, from early colonists to slaves on southern plantations to the landlords of today, have attracted and managed these birds. As a result, the martins have gone through a "behavioral tradition shift," meaning that they have basically learned that nesting near humans is, for one reason or another, beneficial to them.

Why? Perhaps predators are less likely to attack martins when they are near people and houses, or the cavities found in artificial housing are superior to those found in the wild.

Most likely, however, the reason for this change in behavior is that martins have capitalized on the opportunities, in a colonial setting, to copulate with more than one mate. This can benefit males by enabling them to have more offspring, and females by adding genetic diversity to their clutch.

Why Did Humans First Offer Housing for Martins?

Native Americans who attracted martins thou-

A large lakeside gourd colony. Large colonies like this are abundant in the South, where martins have been attracted and managed longer than anywhere else.

sands of years ago probably not only enjoyed the active birds, as we do now, but used these gregarious swallows to their benefit as well. Purple Martins tend to mob and harass large birds, including raptors and vultures. This may have come in handy when people were drying hides and meats and wanted to protect them from birds and other pests. Any investigating raccoons, vultures, or crows would undoubtedly have been harassed if they were close to martins, especially during the incubation and nestling phases. This may have helped establish a tradition among certain tribes that continued for many years.

There are accounts of early European colonists attracting martins as well, using both gourds and multicompartment wooden houses. Some say that early colonial travelers often judged the quality of an inn by the health of its Purple Martin colony.

Over the years, the martins have gradually nested more frequently in human made housing and less frequently in natural cavities. This has continued up to the present, when eastern martins now nest almost exclusively in human-provided housing.

With the introduction of inexpensive, easy-to-use aluminum housing in the 1960s, attracting martins became a widespread hobby and passion. It has continued to grow as an extremely popular activity.

Thus, over time, the lives of humans and Purple Martins have become entwined. As a landlord, you are part of a long line of people, starting thousands of years ago, who have attracted Purple Martins and enjoyed the birds' presence in their lives.

Resources

National Societies

There are two national organizations that are committed to Purple Martins — the Purple Martin Conservation Association and The Nature Society.

Other national groups that can be of help include Audubon societies and other wildlife or bird education/conservation groups, and government agencies like the U.S. Fish and Wildlife Service and the Canadian Wildlife Service.

Yes, birds yawn. Watching martins as they do their daily activities can reveal a number of adorable postures and actions to the patient observer.

Purple Martin Conservation Association (PMCA) — The PMCA is a nonprofit, tax-exempt, international organization devoted to the conservation of Purple Martins. The group advocates, sponsors, and conducts research using the latest in wildlife management techniques and is widely respected as one of the premier sources for information on martins. The PMCA provides information for scientists and backyard landlords alike and dedicates a lot of time and energy toward educating the public about martins.

The *Purple Martin Update* is a quarterly magazine sent to members and includes scientific articles, numerous up-to-date tips on how to be a responsible and active Purple Martin landlord, and many beautiful color photographs of martins. Every issue contains two sections — "The Doctor's House Calls" and "Landlord Letters" — that are open forums for landlords across the country who have questions they want answered or who just want to share their experiences. In addition, the PMCA offers an extensive mail-order catalog featuring a complete list of houses and accessories for Purple Martin landlords.

James R. Hill III, an ornithologist, founded this group in 1986 and has been the executive director ever since.

Purple Martin Conservation Association
Edinboro University of Pennsylvania
Edinboro, PA 16444
Phone: (814) 734-4420
Fax: (814) 734-5803
E-mail: jhill@vax.edinboro.edu

The Nature Society — The Nature Society is an organization founded by J. L. Wade, author of *What You Should Know About the Purple Martin* and *Attracting Purple Martins,* and president of Nature House, Inc. He is also manufacturer of the most complete line of aluminum housing for martins. He pioneered this field in the 1960s and since then has done an enormous amount of work to promote the popularity of the Purple Martin.

The Nature Society is a nonprofit corporation that dedicates itself to the conservation and advancement of native North American songbirds, especially those that are dependent on humans for housing, like the Purple Martin.

Nature Society News is published monthly and contains information on martins and other wildlife, especially birds. It includes columns from different writers and many reader responses. It does a superb job of providing a supportive and informative community of martin landlords and bird enthusiasts.

The Nature Society
Purple Martin Junction
Griggsville, IL 62340
Phone: (217) 833-2323

Regional Societies

In addition to national societies, there are many regional societies for Purple Martins. They are listed below with their addresses. In general, you do not have to live in the region to join the society.

American Bird Conservation Association
Route 3, 111–2nd B Road
Nappanee, IN 46550

Association des Amateurs d'Hirondelles du Quebec
1595 Toscanini
Brossard, QC J3W 3H9
Phone: (514) 464-6094

Conservancy Purple Martin Society
3090 55th Terrace, S.W.
Naples, FL 34116-8034
E-mail: billd@naples.net

Manitoba Purple Martin Club
Box 36 GRP 615 SS6
Winnipeg, MAN R2C 2Z3

National Wildlife Refuge, Inc.
[Formerly "Swallow Project"]
Box 7066
Metairie, LA 70010-7066

The Purple Martin and Bird Society of South Eastern New Brunswick
54 Tower Drive
Dieppe, NB E1A 2G8

The Purple Martin Society, N.A.
Purple Martin Society of Illinois
8921 Royal Drive
Burr Ridge, IL 60521-8332
Phone: (630) 655-2028
E-mail: CDWF38B@Prodigy.com or
Tsuchma@aol.com

On-Line Services

Terry Anne Suchma has been a landlord for many years and has done an enormous amount of work to help raise the level of Purple Martin knowledge. Through her services via the Internet (rec.birds) and bulletin board forums on Prodigy and America Online, she provides personal, invaluable information, advice, and tips to computer-oriented landlords all over the country. On Prodigy, you can find her bulletin board by *jumping* "Hobbies Bulletin Boards," then selecting "birding" and "Purple Martin Society." On America Online, you can reach her forum by going to the "Nature Conservancy Forum," selecting "all birding boards," then "birding by species," then "Purple Martins." You can also reach her directly by E-mail at either CDFW38B@Prodigy.com or Tsuchma@aol.com and by regular mail at 8921 Royal Drive, Burr Ridge, IL 60521-8332.

Manufacturers of Houses and Other Martin Supplies

Andrew M. Troyer
The Birds' Paradise
Route 3, Box 72
Conneautville, PA 16406
Offers wooden houses, plans for wooden houses, House Sparrow and starling traps.

Carroll Industries
Box 577
Madison, MS 39110
Phone: (800) 356-2062
Offers artificial gourds with mounting racks and poles.

Coates Manufacturing, Inc.
605 W. First Street
Bossier City, LA 71111
Phone: (800) 869-2828

Heath Manufacturing Company
Box 105
140 Mill Street
Coopersville, MI 49404
Phone: (616) 837-8181
Offers aluminum and redwood houses, poles, entrance hole plugs, and porch railings.

Natural Insect Control/Dave Mitchell
Route 2
Stevensville, ONT L0S 1S0
Phone: (905) 382-2904

Offers aluminum housing, natural and artificial gourds, poles, entrance hole plugs, porch railings, owl guards, pole guards, starling and House Sparrow traps, subfloors, perches, dawnsong tape, and mail-order catalog.

Nature House, Inc.
Purple Martin Junction
Griggsville, IL 62340
Phone: (800) 255-2692
Offers aluminum housing, poles, ground sockets, entrance hole plugs, porch railings, porch dividers, owl guards, subfloors, House Sparrow traps, books, and tapes of martins.

North American Bluebird Society
Box 6295
Silver Spring, MD 20916-6295
Phone: (301) 384-2798

A typical wooden house with gourds that is obviously attractive to the martins.

If attracting martins were only this easy. There are so many enthusiastic landlords out there — getting in touch with other martin lovers in your area can provide you with great support and information.

Books

Bent, Arthur Cleveland. 1963. *Life Histories of North American Flycatchers, Larks, Swallows, and Their Allies*. New York: Dover Publications, Inc.

Layton, R. B. 1991. *The Purple Martin*. Valley Lee, MD: Nature Books Publishers.

Pearman, Myrna. 1994. *Nestboxes for Prairie Birds*. Alberta: Ellis Bird Farm.

Ray, James D. 1995. *The Purple Martin and Its Management in Texas*. Texas Parks and Wildlife Department Print Shop.

Rogillio, Carlyle. 1991. *Purple Martin Rehabilitation Manual*. Griggsville, IL: The Nature Society.

Slabaugh, Chris J., Sr. 1994. *Purple Martins: "400" Questions and Answers*. Goshen, IN: GET Printing.

Stokes, Donald and Lillian. 1989. *A Guide to Bird Behavior, Volume III*. Boston: Little, Brown.

Turner, Angela, and Chris Rose. 1989. *Swallows and Martins: An Identification Guide and Handbook*. Boston: Houghton Mifflin.

Wade, J. L. 1966. *What You Should Know About the Purple Martin*. Griggsville, IL: J. L. Wade.

——. 1987. *Attracting Purple Martins*. Griggsville, IL: The Nature Society.

Wolinski, Richard A. 1994. *Enjoying Purple Martins More*. Marietta, OH: BWD Press.

Roosts

These are two of the largest known Purple Martin roosts. They can be fun to visit.

Lake Pontchartrain — There are two roosts, each located at one end of the Lake Pontchartrain Causeway. There is a viewing platform at the southern roost that provides observers with spectacular views of the gathering martins. This roost is active throughout the breeding season and reaches its peak from mid-June to mid-July. Lake Pontchartrain is located in southern Louisiana, just north of Metairie, a suburb of New Orleans.

Lake Murray — Martins gather on Lunch Island in Lake Murray, near Columbia, South Carolina. This has recently been made into a sanctuary and is accessible only by boat.

Nest Record Chart

Compartment or Gourd #	Age of Male/Female	Date 1st Egg Is Laid	Earliest Possible Fledging	Date of Nest Check (every 5–7 days)								Totals		
												# of Eggs	# of Nestlings	# of Fledglings
												Totals		

This is a sample nest record chart. In the far left column place the identification number or letter of each gourd or house compartment. In the first shaded column indicate the age of the male and female attending the nest as either A for adult or S for subadult. In the second shaded column record the date the first egg is laid; since eggs are laid 1 per day you can easily calculate when the first egg was laid if you check the box every other day during egg laying. For example, if you find 3 eggs, the first was laid 2 days earlier. In the third shaded column put the date that young from that nest could first leave; you calculate this by adding the number of eggs in the clutch to 41 and then counting that many days from when the first egg was laid. For example, if there were 5 eggs in the clutch and the first egg was laid May 1, then the earliest a young would fledge would be June 15 (5+41 = 46; 46 days after May 1 is June 15). In the next clear columns place the date of your nest check at the top and in the boxes below record whether there is a nest (N) and then the number of eggs (E) or young (Y) in the nest. In the shaded boxes to the right place the totals for each nest. At the very bottom you can record the grand totals for the season.